Education for a Change

D0632597

This challenging, hard-hitting book is about making schooling relevant to modern society. It starts from the premise that our present education system is not equipped to serve students and society in the twenty-first century. In a series of positive, provocative and powerful chapters, the authors look at the critical issues shaping schools today, with a view to:

- set out the critical issues behind the headlines;
- show evidence from research and examples of good practice;
- stimulate public debate and rigorous thinking about how we educate children for life in the twenty-first century;
- provide practical examples of learning for the future;
- present a vision of school transformation.

With contributions from a range of leading commentators, including Tim Brighouse, Jonathon Porritt, Anita Roddick, Charles Handy and Jonathan Sachs, this is a must-read for school leaders, teachers, policy-makers, parents and all education professionals.

Titus Alexander is a Director for Learning Communities at the Scarman Trust.

John Potter is former Director of CSV Education for Citizenship.

Education for a Change

Transforming the way we teach
our children

Edited by
Titus Alexander and John Potter

RoutledgeFalmer
Taylor & Francis Group

LONDON AND NEW YORK

First published 2005 by RoutledgeFalmer
2 Park Square, Milton Park, Abingdon, Oxon, OX14 4RN

Simultaneously published in the USA and Canada
by RoutledgeFalmer
270 Madison Ave, New York, NY 10016

RoutledgeFalmer is an imprint of the Taylor & Francis Group

© 2005 Titus Alexander and John Potter

Typeset in Garamond by Keyword Publishing Services Ltd
Printed and bound in Great Britain by Biddles Ltd, Kings Lynn

British Library Cataloguing in Publication Data
A catalogue record for this book is available from the British Library

Library of Congress Cataloging in Publication Data
A catalog record has been requested

ISBN 0-415-33484-5 (hbk)
ISBN 0-415-33485-3 (pbk)

8/17/11

Contents

Chapter 1

Education for a change

Letter to the reader

Dear reader

About this book

Education for a Change is an invitation to improve children's opportunities for learning. How we, as a society, enable young people to learn is one of our greatest responsibilities. As a society, we have chosen to invest in schools as the main place where children learn what they need to know. This book argues that schools need to change dramatically if all children are to fulfil their potential. We also need to invest in less formal places of learning, particularly families, libraries, museums and active learning centres of all kinds.

Every *Tract* – for that, strictly is what they are – draws on years of experience and thought to propose constructive answers to the question, 'How do we teach our children?'

But this book does not propose a blueprint of solutions. Blueprints and imposed solutions are part of the problem. What we want is a process of discussion and transformation which creates a culture of constant learning and development that radically improves the everyday education of young people. We therefore invite you to:

- Read all or the part that catches your eye, and follow-up the suggestions for further study and action.
- Give this book to other people to read and discuss.
- Form **reading groups**, of parents, governors, teachers and others to discuss it, section by section.
- Form **action groups**, in school, the LEA, your union or professional association, to develop specific suggestions.
- Use the book to start or join the debate in your local area, the press or on the Internet.
- Discuss the issues with your local school governors, your elected councillors and your Members of Parliament, and work with them to transform schools into places of learning capable of equipping young people to thrive in the twenty-first century.

Each section concludes with a list of recommendations. The book finishes with a number of action points for pupils, parents, teachers, governors, LEAs, professional associations, the media, business and government.

This book is therefore an invitation to join the debate, listen to the arguments and make your voice heard. We hope that the ideas discussed here will inspire you to discuss them with friends and colleagues; to work with others to improve and extend learning for young people; and to join a movement that is beginning to transform schools into local centres for lifelong learning.

Everyone has a part to play in improving learning and schools. We hope this book helps us, as individuals and members of society, fulfil our responsibilities for the young people of tomorrow.

Titus Alexander and John Potter
Editors

Tract 1

The battle of ideas

Titus Alexander and John Potter, the Editors, explore the battle for ideas about the future of our schools which must respond to the needs of the present rather than the patterns of the past

We are in the middle of a battle of ideas about schools. The outcome will shape our country for a generation or more. The debate begins with education's role in meeting the needs of young people in a world of constant change.

The world has already changed dramatically over the past century, largely as a result of our use of knowledge in the form of science, technology, medicine, politics, economics and other disciplines. In 1900, almost a third of jobs were in manufacturing and 11% in agriculture. Today less than 2% work in agriculture, just 14% in manufacturing and most jobs are in services. Less than a third of the paid workforce was women; today it is almost half. Most people now live 30 to 40 years longer than in 1900. Increased efficiency and longevity mean that most people today can expect to spend just 20% of their adult waking lives at work and 80% in leisure and learning, whereas 150 years ago most people toiled 80% of their adult waking lives and enjoyed just 20% free time. In material terms, most people in the West are much better off than a century ago. Spending on leisure is now the second largest item of household budgets, after housing. Almost everyone has instant access to news and entertainment through television. Many homes have more information on tap through the Internet than most universities held in their libraries just 20 years ago.

Britain is now a nation of many cultures, faiths, peoples and traditions. It is part of the European Union, the world's largest economic power with 480 million people, 25 member states and a single market in which people have a right to travel and work anywhere from Glasgow to Gdansk. It belongs to the Commonwealth, United Nations and several thousand international organisations and treaties which govern the world. It is part of a global economy, in which the vast productive capacity of China and South East Asia is growing 5 to 10% a year, slashing the price of consumer goods.

Our governments have agreed rules of world trade, which mean that people in Britain compete with people in India paid one-tenth of the amount, in accounting and computing as well as manufacturing.

Over the past century, humanity's ability to wage war killed over 100 million people. Western Europe has sustained over 50 years of peace after four centuries in which every generation fought somewhere on European soil. Today the threats of climate change, terrorism and other dangers have led the Astronomer Royal, Professor Sir Martin Rees, to warn that 'humanity is more at risk than at any earlier phase in its history'. In *Our Final Century: A Scientists Warning* (Rees 2003),[1] he estimates that our chance of survival may only be 50:50. Some of these issues are addressed in school through the citizenship curriculum and the government's Action Plan for Sustainable Development Education. But these remain marginal to mainstream policy and practice.

Knowledge and skill have played a powerful part in both the achievements of the past century and also in its catastrophes. Educated people led the genocides in Germany during the Second World War and Rwanda in 1994. Educated people created machines and chemicals that caused disasters like thalidomide, asbestos and environmental pollution. But education and the use of knowledge also enhances our lives, reducing drudgery and mitigating both natural and man-made disasters.

Education is dangerous

It is easy to assume that education, education, education is, by its nature, a good thing. This is clearly false. Education does not necessarily make people better or stop them from doing terrible things. Education can even increase our ability to cause harm. It is not enough, therefore, to call for 'more education' or 'education for its own sake'. It matters what we teach.

Skills and knowledge are powerful tools. How we use them, individually and collectively, depends on our values. But values alone are not enough to ensure that knowledge is not used dangerously. Educated, idealistic people have, at times, committed terrible crimes against humanity in the name of Buddhism, Christianity, Communism, Hinduism, Islam, progress or another noble value system.

How education is used also depends on the organisations which govern how we live, from the family, school and workplace to the United Nations. Organisations embody our collective learning as a species. Their purpose, rules, beliefs and ways of working shape the way individuals behave. Democratic, pluralistic organisations limit the ability of an individual or group to cause harm and increase incentives for people to work for the common good.

But education is also dangerous for any established order, because it can lead to new ideas, new ways of doing things or new confidence in people to stand up for themselves and overthrow or transform the status quo. This is the essence of democratic pluralism, in which people learn what is possible and seek to make it happen, through enterprise, science, politics, art or their daily lives.

(Continued)

(Continued)

> The dangerous power of education therefore depends on democratic citizenship
> to be a force for good. As citizens, we have a profound responsibility to debate and
> decide the purpose of education and the organisations which govern it.

Schools and society

Schools are about more than basic skills and knowledge or success in passing exams. As Bart McGettrick argues in Tract 8, schools are also about the dignity of each person, about *how* we learn and the values underpinning society. The values of our present school system reflect a divided society, with different kinds of school serving people from different social or religious background. Better-off parents can afford to buy the education of their choice. Seven percent of children go to private schools, where classes are small and they are 30 times more likely to get into a top university than someone from a less advantaged background. State schools in affluent areas are also more likely to be better than schools serving poor areas, where conditions are more challenging. The stark fact remains that those in poverty face enormous obstacles. Lack of education, or even an appreciation of the possibilities offered by education, often go hand in hand with deprivation. It is not surprising that 30% of young offenders and half of all adults in prison have difficulty reading and writing.

More fundamentally, the issue is whether we see education simply as a consumer good, which individuals choose for their private benefit, or whether it is also about a shared citizenship in a common society. And if it is about shared citizenship, is it prescribed by central government, or created by members of a school community, in dialogue with the rest of society, as a 'citizenship school' (Tract 28).

Tackling teaching and learning

We need a more coherent approach to the practice of teaching and learning (pedagogy), which takes account of new discoveries about the brain as well as the needs of learners and teachers as people engaged in a common purpose (Chapter 5). These issues form the heart of the book and the debate society needs if we are to address the challenges of the decades ahead.

We need a new framework for schools, which enables schools to innovate and respond to a changing world in ways that all young people can flourish. In Chapter 4 we explore a variety of ways in which schools are already beginning to interact with their communities in fresh and creative ways. Tim Brighouse (Tract 24) describes how the 'collegiate academy' could meet this challenge in urban areas. Phil Street explores the prospective importance of 'extended schools' and Roz Bird describes how some schools are contributing to the development of rural areas. The section ends with a visionary description of a school of the future by Tony Hinckley (Tract 29)

But three things are likely to be central for children's education in future:

1   Support for parents as a child's first and most enduring educator and families as foundations of life long learning.
2   The critical role of teacher – someone who enables young people to achieve their best. As society becomes more complex and demanding, many different kinds of teachers will become even more important as guides through the avalanche of knowledge and possibilities. There are, of course, many different kinds of teacher, including the parent, grandparent, community coach, mentor, workplace adviser, trainer, youth worker, etc.
3   Learning communities, groups of people learning together in places designed to support learning, whether they are called schools, community learning centres or something else.

These are big questions, to which there are many different answers. But in the battle for ideas there are many different answers about how to achieve our goals. Protagonists in the debate can be grouped into three broad camps:

• **Traditionalist**, who want good discipline, high academic standards and 'a return to the traditional idea of the teacher teaching the class' advocated by Chris Woodhead. 'The belief that teachers must cater for individual needs … is a dangerous nonsense.'[2]
• **Functionalist**, who emphasise skills and employability, as much of this Government's policies have done. They emphasise standards in basic skills of reading, writing, maths and information technology. As set out in the Government's Primary Strategy, it is 'focused on individual pupils' needs and abilities' in order to reach centrally determined targets.
• **Holist**, who are concerned with the whole person and learning in a community, society and the wider world. They recognise learning as a collective process as well as an intensely personal one, in which individual potential is realised as a member of society.

Advocates of each approach extol the best examples of their position and denounce the worst of the others as typical. The truth is that at their best all three approaches are excellent, and the best teachers in each approach use methods associated with the others when appropriate.

Each approach has standards, but they focus on different aspects of human potential. The first concentrates on academic abilities; the second stresses skills for life and work; while the third is more rounded, giving attention to each person as a member of society and their unique potential to develop personal, social and intellectual abilities in a changing world.

The traditionalist, functionalist and holistic views have different objectives. These differences imply real choices. The broad approach of this book supports the holist view and we shall return to these three views at relevant points throughout the book and its conclusions.

In addition to these three approaches, there are three distinct views about how schools should be directed:

- **Market-driven**, as advocated by James Tooley and others (Tooley 2003),[3] believe that parental freedom and choice drives up standards, fosters responsibility and has a wide range of other benefits.
- **State-run**, as exist in most Western societies, often to a standard and curriculum set by the state. Most supporters of state education argue that markets perpetuate social inequality which can be overcome through public provision of schools for all.
- **Pluralist** approaches seek to combine elements of public provision and personal choice to bring about the kind of society we want.

This book does not discuss these differences in detail, but most contributors argue for some form of pluralism within a state-funded framework.

We do not prescribe a blueprint for schools. What we want is groundswell of innovation and improvement from the bottom up, with teachers, parents, students, governors and local people sharing ideas and experiences about the kind of education, places of learning and society they want. This process of transformation is vital, not just for schools, but for the future of this country and the world.

Schools today are a central institution among many different places for learning, including homes, libraries and the Internet. Whether schools still exist 50 years from now will depend on how their ability to transform themselves in response to a world that is changing faster and more unpredictably than anyone can presume to know.

In the battle of ideas, a holistic, pluralistic approach to supporting parents, teachers and learners, in all their diversity, is more likely to give every child a better start in life than the exclusively traditionalist, functionalist, statist or market-driven models being advocated by others.

We are encouraged that some of the policies and language about schools are beginning to go this way as well. But this journey has barely begun, and you, our readers, have a key role in shaping the local and national framework of how we educate our children in a world of change.

Notes

1 *Our Final Century: A Scientists Warning* – How terror, error, and environmental disaster threaten humankind's future, OUP, 2003.
2 Chris Woodhead, *Class War*, Little, Brown, 2002, p. 79.
3 James Tooley, Pauline Dixon and James Stanfield, 2003, *Delivering Better Education: Market solutions for educational improvement*, Adam Smith Institute; James Tooley, *Reclaiming Education*, Cassell, 2000.

Tract 2

How will we educate young people in 2050?

Professor Tim Brighouse, London Commissioner for Schools, offers us his reflections on the future of schools. This tract is based on his lecture to the RSA on Wednesday, 18 October 2000

By 2050 people will look and marvel at the modesty of our ambition and the primitive nature of our present knowledge, and with deep gratitude for our present teachers.

When we celebrated the centenary of the 1870 Education Act, classrooms would have been recognisable to a Victorian time-traveller. Not so in some of today's schools where integrated learning systems see pupils, who have ready access to plentiful computers, accessing their personal files and via their school intranet, a wealth of library materials unimaginable even 30 years ago.

Nanotechnology, which deals with the manipulation of individual atoms and molecules, is accelerating what is possible. In the mid twenty-first century teachers will remember fondly the early electronic whiteboards, the stuttering video links, the primitive computer-assisted learning programmes and the prototype e-books. By 2050, the recently created e-learning foundation will be richer than the wealthiest of the city's medieval guilds and its mission to fund the spread of e-learning devices and research into what works will have reaped a rich harvest.

> *There are two waves of technological advance – of learning and communication – that have combined to change the context of what is educationally possible. They will enable us to close the gap between the haves and the have-nots in a way the book alone never did.*

In 2001 I visited Cape Town, where the sumptuous surroundings of the former all-white, now mixed-race, high schools would turn our best city technology colleges green with envy. Ten miles away, however, the ramshackle shed and the upturned ship's container with no electricity, windows, or floor are home to 350 black children of a shanty town.

In Britain, the gulf may be narrower. But to teach in an affluent suburban or county town, let alone the private sector, is to have the wind at your back, while to do so in cramped surroundings in deprived urban areas requires prodigious energy and cheerful determination in the face of adversity, not to mention extra helpings of generosity of spirit. These contrasts between different areas may still be there in 2050 but other things are sure to change.

Where and how young people learn in 2050 will depend partly on the possibilities created by new discoveries and inventions; partly on economic and political conditions; and overwhelmingly on the decisions we make now, as a society, about schools as institutions.

Here are five predictions about schools of the future:

First, in the light of research into the brain and theories of learning, teachers' questioning techniques will have moved beyond traditional methods. By then, they will be exploiting the *alter ego* dimension of teaching whereby they create an alternative persona to 'unlock the mind and open the shut chambers of the heart'. Evident first in the adventures of teddy bears and in the puppet theatres in infant and nursery schools, the technique is used by secondary drama, history and science teachers who make common cause in the use of masks and glove puppets to create alternative viewpoints. E-tutoring offers many further possibilities in extending this strategy.

Second, by 2050 we shall have extended our expertise in reducing the risks and barriers which some children face at different ages. Tom Wylie, chief executive of the National Youth Agency, referred to the adolescent's 'shame of being a beginner'. Now talented Key Stage 3 teachers are extending their repertoire of suitable techniques to overcome such barriers to learning. There are many more at different ages and stages.

Third, we shall have acknowledged the importance of multiplying the 'specialness opportunities' – that is, the number of relationships created by teachers, support learning staff, peer tutors and mentors to increase the likelihood of the learner feeling so 'special and unique' that they suspend disbelief and make great learning strides. So all staff will offer 'additionality' – for example, their love of photography or music, to extend the chances of success for everyone.

The other two predictions relate to the circumstances in which teachers will operate. The voice of the educator will have dominated the first 50 years of the 'age of learning technology and creativity', just as the voice of the landowner and the industrialist have done in previous ages. In that future time the teacher will be seen as key to society's health and survival.

But that leads to my final prediction. There will be half as many teachers paid three times as much; child/adult ratio of 6 or 7:1.

How can this happen? The signs are already there. Ask any good primary practitioner and they will say they would rather have a trained learning assistant than a slightly smaller class. Teaching assistants, teaching associates, resident and visiting artists and scientists and business people, not to mention personal fitness mentors, will be part of the cast orchestrated by the expert, highly paid teacher.

By 2050, people will look back and marvel at the modesty of our ambition and the primitive nature of our present knowledge. But they will be deeply grateful for the amazing commitment of our present generation of teachers, who have prepared the ground for the next leap forward in educational standards.

Tract 3

What is the government up to?

Toby Greany, former Policy Director, Campaign for Learning, and Cath Jones, Education Researcher, Demos, explore the developments and priorities in government education policy since 1997

Introduction

'Education, education, education': there can be no doubt that New Labour has put a tremendous amount of energy into fulfilling its 1997 election mantra. This tract summarises the key initiatives and developments in schools policy since 1997 and highlights how Labour's thinking has evolved as well as some of the issues and tensions that remain at the heart of the reform process. There are two parts: Part 1 An overview of trends since 1997; Part 2 A summary of specific initiatives.

PART I AN OVERVIEW OF TRENDS SINCE 1997

Government policy under New Labour is driven by the Comprehensive Spending Review (CSR) cycle every three years, in which the Treasury allocates resources to individual departments. Treasury funding is linked to Public Service Agreement (PSA) targets (see Table 1).

Following the Comprehensive Spending Review in 2002, the Department for Education and Skills (DfES) set out its own comprehensive objectives[1] for the following five years.

- **Objective 1:** Give children an excellent start in education so that they have a better foundation for future learning.
- **Objective 2:** Enable all young people to develop and to equip themselves with the skills, knowledge and personal qualities needed for life and work.
- **Objective 3:** Encourage and enable adults to learn, improve their skills and enrich their lives.

In 2004, these objectives became more holistic, focusing on child protection, general well-being, improving skills and breaking cycles of deprivation. Several targets are also shared with the Sure Start Unit and the Departments for Work and Pensions, Health or Culture, Media and Sport.

- Objective 1: Safeguard children and young people, improve their life outcomes and general well-being, and break cycles of deprivation.
- Objective 2: Raise standards and tackle the attainment gap in schools.
- Objective 3: All young people to reach age 19 ready for skilled employment or higher education.
- Objective 4: Tackle the adult skills gap.
- Objective 5: Raise and widen participation in higher education.

The Government's approach to reform

The Treasury's Public Service Agreement targets determined the direction of travel, and the DfES decided the mode of transport. This led initially to a highly prescriptive approach: schools were given their targets, told how to meet them. The National Literacy and Numeracy Strategies, launched shortly after the 1997 election, was a clear example of this approach.

More recently, however, there has been a significant shift in emphasis. The Key Stage 3 Strategy, launched in 2001, was less prescriptive and sought to help teachers understand the implications for good practice, rather than telling them how to 'teach by numbers'. Since 2002, there is a new emphasis on innovation, networks, and 'value added' data on school performance (as opposed to raw test result performance tables).

In May, 2003, Education Secretary Charles Clarke eased the pressure on targets in his reform strategy for primary schools called *Excellence and Enjoyment*. The word 'enjoyment' is itself significant in highlighting creativity and assessment *for* learning (rather than assessment *of* learning). 'Transformation', rather than simply 'reform', had become the keynote of change, which now included an emphasis on structural change[2] in the way schools are organised.[3]

The Department had now turned its attention to teaching and learning alongside the need for system-wide change. A set of Core Principles[4] set out the learner-centred approach to education that most teachers and researchers would support. The emphasis had now moved to engaging pupils in powerful, social learning experiences in schools where the leadership is focused on teaching and learning. In this context it should become possible for targets and Ofsted to inform and enrich, rather than drive the learning process.

PART 2 A SUMMARY OF SPECIFIC INITIATIVES

Primary schools

The **National Numeracy and Literacy Strategies** were launched in 1998. They aim to raise standards at primary level and are attached to ambitious

Table 1   Comprehensive Spending Review 2002

Objective 1: Safeguard children and young people, improve their life outcomes and general well-being, and break cycles of deprivation.

1. Improve children's communication, social and emotional development, so that, by 2008, 50% of children reach a good level of development at the end of the Foundation Stage and reduce inequalities between the level of development achieved by children in the 20% most disadvantaged areas and the rest of England.

2. As a contribution to reducing the proportion of children living in households where no-one is working, by 2008:

    *   increase the stock of Ofsted-registered childcare by 10%;
    *   increase the take-up of formal childcare by lower income working families by 50%; and
    *   introduce by April 2005, a successful light-touch childcare approval scheme.

3. Reduce the under-18 conception rate by 50% by 2010, as part of a broader strategy to improve sexual health.

4. Halt the year-on-year rise in obesity among children under 11 by 2010, in the context of a broader strategy to tackle obesity in the population as a whole.

5. Narrow the gap in educational achievement between looked-after children and that of their peers, and improve their educational support and the stability of their lives so that, by 2008, 80% of children under 16, who have been looked after for 2.5 or more years, will have been living in the same placement for at least 2 years, or are placed for adoption.

Objective 2: Raise standards and tackle the attainment gap in schools.

6. Raise standards in English and maths so that:

    *   by 2006, 85% of 11 year olds achieve level 4 or above, with this level of performance sustained to 2008; and
    *   by 2008, the proportion of schools in which fewer than 65% of pupils achieve level 4 or above is reduced by 40%.

7. Raise standards in English, maths, ICT and science in secondary education, so that:

    *   by 2007, 85% of 14 year olds achieve level 5 or above in English, maths and ICT (80% in science) nationally, with this level of performance sustained to 2008; and
    *   by 2008, in all schools at least 50% of pupils achieve level 5 or above in each of English, maths and science.

8. Improve levels of school attendance, so that, by 2008, school absence is reduced by 8%, compared to 2003.

9. Enhance the take-up of sporting opportunities by 5 to 16 year olds, so that the percentage of school children in England, who spend a minimum of 2 hours each week on high quality PE and school sport, within and beyond the curriculum, increases from 25% in 2002 to 75% by 2006 and to 85% by 2008, and to at least 75% in each School Sport Partnership by 2008.

Objective 3: All young people to reach age 19 ready for skilled employment or higher education.

10. By 2008, 60% of those aged 16 to achieve the equivalent of 5 GCSEs at grades A* to C; and in all schools at least 20% of pupils to achieve this standard by 2004, rising to 25% by 2006 and 30% by 2008. (This target may be reviewed in light of recommendations in the Tomlinson Report.)

11. Increase the proportion of 19 year olds who achieve at least level 2 by 3 percentage points between 2004 and 2006, and a further 2 percentage points between 2006 and 2008, and increase the proportion of young people who achieve level 3.

12. Reduce the proportion of young people not in education, employment or training, by 2 percentage points by 2010.

Objective 4: Tackle the adult skills gap.

13. Increase the number of adults with the skills required for employability and progression to higher levels of training through:

- improving the basic skill levels of 2.25 million adults between the launch of Skills for Life in 2001 and 2010, with a milestone of 1.5 million in 2007; and
- reducing by at least 40% the number of adults in the workforce who lack NVQ 2 or equivalent qualifications by 2010. Working towards this, one million adults in the workforce to achieve level 2 between 2003 and 2006.

Objective 5: Raise and widen participation in higher education.

14. By 2010, increase participation in higher education towards 50% of those aged 18 to 30 and also make significant progress year on year towards fair access, and bear down on rates of non-completion.

targets for attainment at Key Stage 2. The Numeracy and Literacy Frameworks provide teachers with intensive ongoing professional development, a set of yearly teaching programmes, key objectives and a planning grid. The strategies are not compulsory, but primary schools must show adequate alternative provision if they do not use them. Most local authorities and schools do so. Local authorities also help to co-ordinate a national network of literacy and numeracy advisers.

The aim is to increase the percentage of 11-year-olds achieving Level 4 in the Key Stage 2 English and maths tests. The targets for 2002 were 80% in English and 75% in maths, but the results fell short of the targets.[5] Thus the initial leap in results has reached a plateau. From September 2003 the two strategies have been combined into a single '**National Primary Strategy**' and the Excellence and Enjoyment paper (May 2003) reflects a re-evaluation of the targets strategy.

The **Languages for all, languages for life** programme, announced in December 2002, aims to ensure every pupil aged 7–11 is able to study a European language by the end of the decade, so every pupil has the opportunity to learn a language.

Key Stage 3 (11–14)

In 2002 the Government focused on standards in secondary schools. With standards rising at primary level, a strategy was developed to address the 'dip' in pupil attainment in Key Stage 3. *The Key Stage 3 National Strategy* was launched in September 2002 and covers five curriculum areas:

- Maths
- English
- Teaching and Learning in Foundation Subjects
- ICT
- Science

It provides targeted support to schools and teachers, including lesson planning, resources and model lessons. LEA facilitators and national directors support different subject areas. Professional development training addresses children's different learning needs and introduces cross-curricular learning themes, such as Thinking Skills.

14–19 Phase

Curriculum 2000 aimed to bring greater flexibility and breadth into the post-GCSE curriculum. The Government is now developing a coherent framework for the 14–19 phase of education, which is fragmented between academic and vocational (job-related) routes.

The *14–19 Green Paper*, published early in 2002, proposed more flexibility for learners within a single curriculum framework by strengthening individual 'learning pathways' – including work-based, work-related and college-provided courses.

In January 2003 the Government published *14–19: opportunity and excellence*. Many students in this age group were described as being 'bored', 'feeling trapped' and believing themselves to be 'failures'. The proposals therefore aimed to create a curriculum that addresses the individual needs of 14–19 students within a unified qualifications framework designed to provide:

- a stronger vocational offer;
- assessment which recognises all of the young person's achievements; and
- *broader choice within a unified framework of qualifications.*

It further argued that students with good GCSEs need a broader range of subjects and learning experiences, and students pursuing a vocational track need to be integrated into a wider framework of provision and recognition.

A working group, led by Mike Tomlinson, is developing proposals for a new diploma which is likely to include a general education in English, maths and information technology; specialist subjects related to their interests; and credit for extracurricular activities such as arts or voluntary work. (See Tract 23.)

School inclusion, youth and advisory services

In its first term the Government introduced ambitious targets to cut **school exclusions**, but the difficulties of achieving targets for both inclusion and attainment have prompted a more flexible approach. New support services exist to prevent disaffection, encourage young people's educational and personal aspirations, and support schools in managing behaviour. This has been accompanied by reforms to the criminal justice system, such as Youth Offending Teams.

For schools, new regulations and guidelines on exclusion took effect in January 2002. Currently 34 LEAs are participating in Behaviour Improvement Projects (BIP) designed to provide integrated frameworks to help schools reduce exclusions.[6]

In addition, **youth services**, run by local authorities, voluntary organisations and others have received extra resources to improve quality and co-ordination.[7]

The Government will increase Local Authority Education Budgets by 5.9% and invest a further £54 million in modernising services to meet these new expectations.

Connexions is a new support service for all young people aged 13–19 in England. It aims to provide integrated advice, guidance and access to personal development opportunities to help young people make a smooth transition to adulthood and working life. Connexions advisers provide personal advice and access to educational opportunities for young people from secondary school onwards. The service is targeted at young people facing particular risk, but is also universally available.

Diversity and innovation across all schools

New Labour has sought to stimulate **innovation** in many different ways. Area-based initiatives aim to bring schools together in finding innovative ways to tackle their problems and improve standards.

- **Education Action Zones** (EAZs) were an early attempt to establish collaborative networks of schools and attract new sources of funding and support from the private sector. EAZs have produced mixed results, and the overall programme was partially superseded by Excellence in Cities (see below). The policy is now being replaced with excellence clusters.
- **Excellence in Cities** (EiC) aims to address educational problems in major cities. Excellence clusters offer additional support such as City Learning Centres, Learning Support Units, Learning Mentors, extracurricular activities for Gifted and Talented students, and partnerships with Beacon Schools (see below). Originally planned for secondary schools, it now includes primary schools and smaller areas of deprivation.
- The **Specialist Schools** programme is central to the Government's goal to increase diversity and improve standards in secondary education. The Programme helps schools, in partnership with private sponsors and supported by additional Government funding, to establish distinctive identities. It is motivated by a conviction that 'a distinctive ethos and identity' creates high-achieving schools, and that diversity of schools is needed to meet the expectations and needs of learners and parents. Charles Clarke's first major policy announcement as Education Secretary was to set a goal of 1,500 specialist schools by 2005, and make funding available for all secondary schools to eventually become specialist.

A specialist school must raise £50,000 in private sector sponsorship, less if they have fewer than 500 pupils, and prepare four-year development plans. Each receives a one-off £100,000 capital grant and £123 per pupil recurrent funding initially for four years.

Specialist schools focus on their chosen subject area but must meet the full National Curriculum and a broad and balanced education for all pupils. Specialist schools work within a named 'family of schools' for the benefit of pupils beyond their own school boundaries and the wider community by sharing of good practice and expertise.

While specialist schools achieve more highly than others at GCSE and A level, on average, the difference is modest. Ministers are therefore preoccupied with how to use expertise to support improvement across larger numbers of schools. (See also Tract 23, 'Winners and losers')

- Similarly, **Beacon schools** provide examples of replicable successful practice. They offer advice on a wide range of areas including subjects, pupil monitoring, management, provision for gifted and talented children, parent involvement, special needs and anti-bullying strategies.[8]

  With the **Advanced schools programme** from April 2003, the Department is reviewing the Beacon school programme to ensure that it 'continues to offer the most effective means of delivering its objectives'. Beacon schools have helped schools they work with, but there remains a question whether this model of 'knowledge transfer' is effective.

- **City Academies** are publicly funded independent schools set up and run by sponsors, who provide up to 20% of capital costs, with the Government providing the balance and recurrent costs. There are 25 in total, with more than 50 planned by 2007, funded by taxpayers after initial cash injection by private sponsors. City Academies provide free education and state-of-the-art facilities to secondary age pupils of all abilities, including provision for children with special educational needs. They aim to offer a broad and balanced curriculum including a specialism.

- The **Innovation Unit** has been set up within the DfES to foster innovation. It is responsible for administering the powers which allow schools to disapply (with Ministerial approval) statutory requirements in the interests of innovative ways of raising standards.

Workforce reform

The 2001 election manifesto committed the Government to employ at least 10,000 extra teachers, 20,000 extra non-teaching staff and 1,000 trained bursars by 2006. Since then the challenges of recruitment and retention in education have become even sharper. Initial Teacher Training recruitment has increased through recruitment drives and bursaries for trainees. A 'Fast Track' training programme has been developed for trainees with potential to become advanced practitioners or future school leaders.

The DfES also aims to increase numbers of Teaching Assistants and support staff beyond the manifesto targets to reduce workload for teachers and free-up time for priority activities. By 2006 there should be 50,000 new support staff in schools.

The DfES *Strategy for Continuing Professional Development*, published in October 2002, was developed with the General Teaching Council, includes school-based development as well as external activities. The GTC Professional Learning Framework outlines opportunities and resources teachers should have a right to. A **National College for School Leadership** has also been set up to give heads and managers high quality training.

In January 2003 the Government signed a 'historic' *workforce agreement* with most of the main teaching unions. The agreement aims to reduce teachers' working hours over the next four years to ensure all teachers do less administration and have guaranteed planning, preparation and assessment time within the school day. The agreement is backed by all professional associations apart from the NUT.

Conclusion

These initiatives give a sense of the breadth and ambition of the Government's reform agenda. It faces huge challenges, attempting to transform the school system at the same time as reassuring schools, parents, the media and, perhaps most importantly, the Treasury, that it can safeguard standards. There are many who remain unconvinced. On one side are those who call for more traditional teaching. On the other are those who know that schools turn children off learning unless they become exciting, learner-centred environments where children *want* to go. When children are as keen to learn as they are to play, then we will really see 'Education, education, education'.

Notes

1 *Investment for Reform and Education and Skills: Delivering Results – A Strategy to 2006*, 2001.
2 *Education Epidemic: transforming secondary schools through innovation networks*, by David Hargreaves, DEMOS 2003.
3 *A New Specialist System: Transforming Secondary Education*, launched by Charles Clarke early in 2003.
4 *Core Principles for Teaching and Learning, School Improvement and System-wide Reform*, DfES Standards and Effectiveness Unit in February 2003.
5 Results were 75% in English and 73% in maths.
6 Other initiatives include the behaviour and attendance strand of the Key Stage 3 Strategy; Excellence in cities and excellence clusters; and further recent agreement with LEAs to ensure permanently excluded pupils receive a full-time education.
7 *Transforming Youth Work: Resourcing Excellent Youth Services* (December 2002), sets out expectations of local authorities in co-ordinating and developing youth services.
8 Some provide support through Initial Teacher Training or work with newly qualified teachers. Others work with failing schools or schools on special measures.

Tract 4

Key questions

The editors invite you to wrestle with these questions as you read the book

1   Who is the young person in class, on the street, in your home? What does she want and need from you, as a person? What fills her with joy and what fears conceal her? Where is her courage, and what hurt does she hide? What and how does she see? What does she have to say? What does she know about the world and how does she learn? Can you really teach her before you know her?
2   What challenges will young people face as they grow up?
3   What values, knowledge, skills and abilities will young people need to thrive in this changing, uncertain world? How much should young people decide for themselves what to learn, and how much should we guide them; how much should they learn from history and the great literature, art and science of the past, and how much should they be orientated towards their future and the world that is being transformed around us?
4   How can they best be inspired to learn in-depth as well as breadth, and to sustain their commitment to learning throughout their lives?
5   How do we – educators, parents, employers, friends – develop the kind of skills and qualities needed to inspire and sustain learning in depth?
6   What is the special role of school, if any, given the growth in other means of learning? And how should schools evolve to fill that role?
7   And how do we enable *all* young people to use and enjoy the wealth of educational opportunities other than school?
8   Last but not least, how do we support parents and carers as children's first and most enduring educators?

AGENDA FOR CHANGE

In this chapter we examined the battle for ideas in education and Tim Brighouse's vision of schools in 2050, together with a summary of Government initiatives in 2004.

The key points for action are:

- To develop a holistic approach to education at all levels, which 'unlocks the mind and opens the heart'.
- To apply our understanding of learning and how the brain works to develop a wide range of learning methods, including story, performance, projects and e-learning.
- To reduce the risks and barriers faced by some children and ensure that every child has the attention and support she or he needs to achieve their potential in life.
- To multiply opportunities for each child to develop their unique talents by enabling *all* staff and other adults to offer their special skills and passions for pupils to learn.
- To steadily increase the average child/adult ratio to 7:1.
- To give schools and communities greater control over how they integrate and apply national initiatives.
- To secure adequate funding and support for schools.
- To create a coherent, comprehensive and flexible framework of national policy which enables all schools to focus their energies on children's learning.

Chapter 2

The case for change

Dear Parents and Guardians

What is education for?

As parents and guardians we are the single most important influence in the upbringing of our children. Recent research among 3,000 children showed that parents' involvement in their children's education has a bigger effect on their success in school than any other factor.[1] The way we treat our children, what we expect of them, and the ways in which we nurture, support and challenge them will, for good and ill, shape them for life. (See Tract 12.)

Our primary role as parents is to build relationships with our children around which they can grow, test themselves, stumble and flourish as they make a place for themselves in the world. This relationship is rooted in our values and the ways we engage with a world where traditional values are challenged and new values are emerging. As parents, consciously and unconsciously, we pass on to our children our values as well as our material possessions.

Finally, we share something of what we know and what we can do with our children. We teach our children to play football, cook, shop, sing, sew and make things. We may share with them our passion for dancing, drama or drumming. We may even stimulate in them a love of languages, science or maths. It is in these areas that we are likely to be most conscious of our limits, and most aware that we need to work with others, including friends, neighbours, schools and across the community. And so we return to our question: What is education for?

We begin by setting out the case for a change in education. We follow this up with reflections on the purpose of education and the role of schools by two experienced and eminent commentators. We conclude with a response from a headteacher who is excited by what has already been achieved and clear about where we need to go next.

The vision of 'education for a change' will be realised only if it enjoys the active involvement of parents, pupils and everyone with a passionate interest in the well-being of our children.

John Potter and Titus Alexander

Note

1 *The Impact of Parental Involvement, Parental Support and Family Education on Pupil Achievement and Adjustment: A Literature Review*, by Professor Charles Desforges, Emeritus Professor, University of Exeter, and Dr Leon Feinstein, London School of Economics, which can be downloaded, free, from www.dfes.gov.uk

Tract 5

A quick case for change

Tony Hinckley, educator, adviser and writer, introduces our examination of the case for change with a quick summary of the key points that we shall explore further in subsequent tracts

- We have a pass–fail examination system that is, by definition, exclusive not inclusive.
- Children develop at different rates and in different ways yet we test them at the same age and in the same way.
- Our education system (including some or even much of the teaching that goes on) is predicated on a view of intelligence as a single fixed commodity.
- The amount of information increases daily and at an ever-increasing rate, yet we continue to value the testing of content and memory.
- Demotivation of young people at all levels of attainment is built into our school system.
- Community education does not build on school education but aims at remediating it.
- Our education system is damaging to the self-esteem of the majority of young people.

Tract 6

Time for a change

John Potter, Editor, explores the background to the case for change

Our education system has changed remarkably little over the past hundred years. Visitors from the Victorian age would readily recognise a modern classroom with children at their desks in rows sitting in front of the teacher who is busy telling them what they should know. Some identify – with gratified amusement – the buildings in which they themselves had studied. Others sigh with dismay at the poor quality of twentieth-century school buildings.

A few of our visitors, however, while looking round our most pioneering institutions, voice amazement at what they find. Children study attentively in independent learning centres; teachers use interactive whiteboards in class-rooms that bear little resemblance to their Victorian equivalents; adults and visitors to the school work alongside pupils as mentors and fellow learners. Children take part in staff appointments, review the curriculum and make recommendations to the governors for the use of the suspended timetable during citizenship week. Pupils and staff alike have digital access to the biggest collection of data that the world has ever known. Personal learning plans are developed for each student in the context of a group of 12 schools who belong to a college of institutions offering lifelong learning for the whole community. The young people spend time off-site (or in other buildings on the same site) working with and learning from public services, business and community organisations. The academic curriculum, the ethos and activities of the school and the concerns of the locality are blended to offer each pupil an entitlement to learning through community involvement.

Almost every proposal for effective learning in this book is drawn from real life. Before exploring some of these possibilities in more detail, we need to identify the challenges we currently face. The case for change must be understood and tackled at three levels: 1 society; 2 the school; and 3 the interaction between teacher and pupil.

Tackling social attitudes

Children learn as much from the way we treat them as from lessons. However, we are deeply ambivalent about children. Our attitudes to children are rooted more often in myth rather than in reality. At one moment we see children as innocents and guard them from every real or imagined danger; at the next moment we treat youngsters as monsters from whom society needs protection. Such attitudes serve both children and society badly. Only those with no recollection of the childhood cruelties of the playground or the sports changing room can entertain the illusion that children are unsullied by the rougher ways of the world. The attempt to protect children from every source of harm or danger will create a generation of young people incapable of looking after themselves or others. Society needs to be as actively concerned with fostering children's capacity to look out for themselves as with protecting them against dangers.

Child protection rightly requires the screening of adults directly responsible for their well-being and safety. Revelations of the sexual abuse by care-workers, teachers and clergy make this necessary. The vicious massacre of children in a Dunblane primary school classroom in 1996 emphasised the need for schools to exercise vigilance over visitors and sparked off a national debate over the right of citizens to bear arms. These legitimate concerns should not obscure the fact that children are more at risk from people they know – peers, family and acquaintances – than from strangers. It is better and more effective to teach children the skills and values of mutual care and protection than to isolate them increasingly from the world around them.

Children develop the solutions to most challenges they face. They learn – with adult oversight – to help each other avoid bullying, support each other, and create places where they can safely be alone or seek help over a problem. They also tackle the problem of safe travel to school by taking part in a 'walking bus', a simple scheme whereby with the help of adults young children walk – yes *WALK* – together to school. Treating children as the solution rather than the problem provides the basis for a culture shift in attitudes among teachers, parents and the public. (See also Tract 39, 'Engaging young people in real learning'.)

Children are not angels, but neither are they devils in disguise. Young people, like the rest of us, need the support of a healthy, ordered environment. If this is absent, disruption is likely to ensue. This disruption can poison the lives not only of the children themselves but of whole communities. Experienced teachers are clear about two things. First, children must know exactly where they stand. Secondly, they should share responsibility for the world in which they live.

Oliver Goldsmith Primary School in South London was once described by an Ofsted inspector as 'being like something out of Dante's inferno'.[1] Damilola Taylor attended this school before he was brutally murdered. Oliver

Goldsmith's is now a model of how vision and effective discipline can turn a school round. The new head, Mark Parsons, introduced school rules that are clear, fair and consistently applied. He and his staff are tough. A playground fight triggers a single warning, which, if ignored, is followed by a short suspension. Behaviour has now improved dramatically. Test results have risen and classroom fights and Pokemon protection rackets have become a thing of the past. Similar stories are repeated in schools across the country.

Eroding the territory of childhood

Myths that distort our view of children can foster threats to childhood itself. Richard Reeves[2] argues that 'The territory of childhood is threatened by three main enemies: commercialisation, paranoia and the privatisation of parenting. In each case, the dangers become stronger year by year. And the resistance is ragged.'

There is evidence from the Food Standards Agency that commercial advertising encourages child obesity. MORI research show that parents cite commercial pressure as the single most difficult aspect of raising children today. Mary MacLeod, from the Family and Parenting Institute, points to the damaging effects of 'bullying TV which works by being nasty to people in some way'.

In response to commercial pressure of this kind, Tessa Jowell, Secretary of State for Culture, Media and Sport, advocates education, rather than regulation. In short, government makes teachers responsible for helping children resist the rampant pressures of commerce.

The second threat is from paranoia. Children are more at risk from those they know than from those they don't. The evidence is that violent assaults on children are extremely rare and becoming even rarer.[3] In spite of the facts, however, a year after the murder of 2-year-old James Bulger, 97% of parents saw the possible abduction of their child as their 'greatest fear'.

The third threat follows from the second. With the emphasis on 'stranger danger' we are witnessing the 'privatisation' of parenting. Children are increasingly holed-up in the home or contained in the car. In brief, concludes Reeves, 'we are raising a generation to be fat and fearful … '.

Conclusion 1: Education is more than what happens in schools

A review of education requires us to examine our attitudes towards children and childhood; to promote healthy living and protect children from substance and food abuse; and to offer children a range of positive relationships with adults as well as protecting them from abusive relationship. For this, we need to support parents as a child's most influential educator.

The school

The need for changes to schools is widely agreed, but the solutions are in dispute. Three factors shape society's expectations of schools and the changes they need to make.

- A modern, complex and highly competitive economy requires schools to educate children who are technically competent, socially mature and capable of enterprising solutions to a wide range of (often unpredictable) social, political and technological challenges.
- A twenty-first century democracy requires young people to become informed citizens capable of reflecting on political and social issues, engaging in discussion and taking responsible action. Citizenship education is now part of the national curriculum, but most schools are just beginning to give pupils experience of democratic responsibility and participation in school life.
- A plural community, comprising people from many different ethnic and cultural backgrounds, needs members who are confident in their own identity and able to understand and relate to the cultures of fellow citizens from different backgrounds. The longer-term implications for schools and colleges of policies for social inclusion have scarcely begun.

Over the past 15 years schools have experienced a bewildering range of initiatives designed to tackle these challenges. The problem has been the lack of coherence between these initiatives. On the one hand, the standards agenda has sought (with some success) to drive up academic performance by imposing sets of challenging tests and targets. This has encouraged schools to teach to the test and make league tables the chief determinant of school policy. The evidence suggests that this top-down approach is running out of steam (see Tract 22). On the other hand, the values agenda seeks to build a learning-centred culture where 1 assessment is designed to help pupils learn better; 2 spiritual, moral and cultural values are seen as integral to the whole curriculum; and 3 teachers' professionalism is centre stage (see Chapter 5).

Conclusion 2: Schools require a coherent philosophy of education

The needs of the economy, civil society and a plural society can only be met by a school system that has a coherent philosophy of education that enables young people to think for themselves, participate in decision-making and take responsibility for their actions as members of society.

The interaction between teacher and pupil

The role of the teacher is at the heart of the debate about the future of schools. The view of the teacher as the expert who pours a jug of knowledge into the empty glass of the student's mind is discredited. Learning is more than the exchange of information. Students now have direct access to an unprecedented store of e-learning. In some matters – particularly digital matters – the knowledge and skill of pupils exceed that of their teachers. The task of the educator, then, is not to be omniscient but to be professionally skilled at helping students learn to learn (see Chapter 5).

Conclusion 3: Effective pedagogy is central to the future of education

The task of educators is to 'draw out' their pupils' curiosity about the world, to nourish their achievements, and to equip them for lifelong learning.

Approaching education for a change

People's approach to what changes are needed will depend on how they see the role of schools. They may be *traditionalists, functionalists* or *holists*.

- *Traditionalists* see the contribution of the school in largely academic terms, though many also stress traditional religious and/or social values.
- *Functionalists* focus on the narrower responsibilities of the school to equip children with the *necessary qualifications* for adult and working life. Within the functionalist approach, there is a further tension between *training* (leading to work-related qualifications) and *education* that sets out to enrich and broaden the mind.
- *Holists* emphasise the importance of *motivation, attitudes and relationships* in learning of all kinds and so place great value on a partnership between parents, pupils and teachers. Holists also seek to understand the world as an interconnected whole, not just specialist subjects which are separate from each other and from our lives in the world.

The three approaches may have objectives in common. Holists are as much concerned with standards and achievement as functionalists. The disagreement is often more about means than ends. Traditionalists frequently share the holists' concern with relationships and values in the education; but they are usually more conservative about teaching methods and involving parents and pupils in making decisions about school life.

In what follows, Bart McGettrick offers his vision of the purpose of education and Charles Handy reflects on his own experience to point up the critical challenges faced by schools. Titus Alexander then introduces us to the wider concept of learning families. Between each Tract public figures with an active interest in the future of education – Satish Kumar, Jonathon Porritt and John Monks – offer brief comments on critical issues. We conclude with reflections from a practising headteacher, Elizabeth Allen, who invites her generation of fellow 'baby-boomer' heads to 'seize the day' by confidently leading schools into the changes that they and their pupils deserve.

Notes

1 See The mystery of childhood, Mary Riddell, *Sunday Observer*, 17 March 2002.
2 The battle for childhood, Richard Reeves (cover story), *New Statesman*, 20 October 2003.
3 Between 1988 and 1999 the number of children between 5 and 16 decreased from 4 per million to 3 per million in E&W. The number of under-fives dropped from 12 per million to 9 per million. Cases of abduction where the offender was found guilty dropped from 26 to 8 over the same period. But a year after the murder of 2-year-old James Bulger, 97% of parents saw the possible abduction of their child as their 'greatest fear'.

Tract 7

Education to save the planet

Jonathon Porritt, Programme Director of Forum for the Future, comments on the need to make the connection between schools, learning and the future of the planet

One way or another, we must learn to live sustainably on this planet. It's not optional. In evolutionary terms, you're either in (sustainably) or out (as in 'extinct'). Today's sustainability challenge is, therefore, not if but *when*. So how long will it take – bearing in mind that the longer it takes, the more painful that inevitable reconciliation between humankind and the rest of life on earth will prove to be.

Which makes one think about education somewhat differently! From this evolutionary perspective, the *principal* purpose of our educational system should be to enable young people to meet that challenge – both conceptually and practically. Tear up the curriculum, and start all over again with the biological, physical and spiritual foundations on which an understanding of sustainability rests.

And make every school a working exemplar of sustainable living: carbon-neutral, zero-waste, growing and cooking as much of its own organic food as possible, embedded in the local community, with lots of people (particularly older people) coming into the school to help, and lots of children going out into the community to help, green travel plans, virtual twinning with schools in the developing world, lots of exercise, field trips, visits to farms and theatres, and so on. Sustainability across the curriculum, and embodied in every facet of the school's life.

Tract 8

What is education for?

Bart McGettrick, Professor of Education at Glasgow University, asks the timeless, ageless question

Introduction

'What is education for?' ... is a timeless and ageless question. Neither time nor the wisdom of the responses has rendered this an irrelevant question. Differing contexts and the changing nature of communities, changing expectations, and changing values do not allow the question to be answered with certainty or with permanence.

Among the purposes of education are to raise the dignity of each child, to bring to distinction all children, and indeed all people. Education is concerned with the formation of each person. It forms people

- of love, care, and compassion;
- who appreciate and will create beauty; and
- who have the urge and the abilities to serve others.

This idea of service to others should not be narrowly understood as a functional set of activities alone. For example, some people are born with such disabilities that they mainly serve others by their smiles. We value people for who they are and not for what they can do. One of the key objectives of education must be to form and support people of hope and of dignity. It is through hope that we can have the confidence to transform society. This has to be done as individuals and as a community ... and there is a very strong link between these.

This principle of education being about formation is very important. Education is not a matter of transmission of knowledge or concepts or ideas. It is not essentially about 'information', but about 'formation'.

There are three main areas which we need to consider above all others. We must:

- form the young by involving them with the current norms and conventions of our society; this is particularly concerned with truth, reason, and enterprise;
- teach knowledge and understanding that will help them to serve current society; developing their gifts and ideals to serve the world;
- develop the gifts and abilities of each person, and their capacity to appreciate beauty; this is concerned with creativity, imaginative thinking and 'emotional intelligence'.

Much of what we learn through education arises not from the 'content' – the knowledge, skills, principles and understanding of a subject or topic – but from the ways in which we learn. It has as much to do with *how* we learn as to *what* we learn. Education is the conversation from generation to generation about matters of significance. This is especially true of the values which we learn, or which develop in us. They are not carried by some 'transmission model' of teaching and learning in which the teacher has a value and somehow 'transmits' it to the learner. Values are formed in relationships and are carried in the relationships of life.

Education is a process which changes, moves, is flexible and is infinitely varied. In previous generations there was the likelihood of children learning from parents or adults. That was the basis of education and many of our educational structures and practices derive from that model. For a variety of reasons, including the rapid advancement of technologies, knowledge and changes of attitudes we are facing generations in which we learn much information from our children. We are likely to be learning from generations yet to be born. Of course education is not simply about information and knowledge. It is also about wisdom, creativity and care – aspects less likely to be found in such abundance in younger generations. Education is not a static condition or phenomenon, but one which is related to the changing and fluid cultures of our times. We must believe, fully believe, that by the use of our psychological resources we increase them. It is only by the use of our material resources do we deplete them. Education seeks to increase 'the intellectual capital' of this world.

The means by which we do this are through the curriculum, through what we learn and what we teach, and how that learning takes place. The central purposes of education, however, lie beyond these means alone, beyond a narrow definition of the curriculum. The curriculum is not the purpose of education, but the means of achieving the primary purposes. This conceptualisation of education forms a sharp distinction between means and ends.

The essential principles of education expose people to experiences and the feelings of love, beauty, compassion, goodness, care and the other positive human emotions and feelings. Educational practices should not stop with an awareness of the principles, because without related experience these are empty, and so should bring people to experience these qualities of life, and through these to form their values systems and dispositions in relation to others. It is this experience which currently represents the greatest challenge to education, partly because it is this which leads to the formation of the mind and the person. It is not the words of a concept which are formative, but the experiences which give power and meaning to the person. A culture of learning has to actively engage people in the joy of learning, and the experience of it.

Education therefore values each individual for the gifts and talents which each has, as well as providing a means of empowering each person to contribute to the benefit of all society. At the heart of education is the formation of people of enquiry and intellectual debate. That debate is about much more than knowledge, understanding and skills. At the core of the debate are the values which are held, and which are seen as significant for future generations. It is also about the promotion of imagination and the encouragement towards creative thought and action. These are all based on 'the disciplined mind' and disciplined thinking. They are not alternatives to the disciplines themselves, but, at their best, the result of them.

This opens the debate about whether the dominant aspect of life is rational behaviour, or whether rationality is only a means of explaining the ways in which we deal with our passions. Whatever our views on this our ideas in education must be based on some notion of 'the virtuous person' and a 'better life'. If we are to claim some form of transformation then this must have an idea of 'good' as its guiding principle. This is likely to mean ensuring that the qualities of integrity, honesty, courage, and caring are to the fore in educational provision. It involves being able to learn and re-learn; acting with ethical principles; and having a deep care for oneself and others.

The balance of the self and others is central to this conceptualisation. The need for education to pay attention to the inner self is a vital part of human development. This is not the narrow concerns of the cognitive alone, but is that personal search, a journey of mind and heart, and the capacity for personal transformation which are all so important. It is through this personal transformation that wider influences can be felt and actions taken. The idea of 'making the world a better place' is open to so many interpretations. Education has to be based on the hope of a better society, and the realism of each person contributing to it. Too often there is apathy which prevails and suggests limits to the contribution that education makes to the development of the whole person. The passions and instincts of the person are found in their individual 'good', and in the common good. There is no separation between the person and the communities of which they are part.

The polarity still exists between a world of care, compassion and love, appreciating beauty and serving others; and a world of efficiency, effectiveness, and employment and career development. These are not, and cannot be taken to be the stark alternatives. It is true, however, that professionals in their work must get beyond the politically expedient and the immediate. Ideas of efficiency and effectiveness have to follow the essential ideas of forming people of hope and of service.

The tendency to describe education in terms of outcomes and targets; to turn each perspective into 'a problem', to use the language of the marketplace – is to fail to engage the hearts and souls of those who learn. Forming citizens is as much about restoring and maintaining a sense of passion, joy and motivation as it is about some notion of 'performance'. This is the tension of the dominant aspect of humanity or the human condition being our feelings and passions, or our rational ways of dealing with these.

Yet there can be no doubt that any conception of education which is sustainable in the present world must pay attention to both the individual and the community. It must be 'inclusive' in every way. It must pay attention to

- the needs of its affluent – and especially its poorest;
- those who are fully engaged in civic society and those who are at its margins;
- those who are young as well as those who are elderly;
- those who are healthy and those who are not.

Where there is no inclusion of this kind we are all the poorer for it. This is the need to build 'cultural capital'. Participation in democracy must therefore focus on relationships and processes and not only on outcomes and products. One of the major difficulties that teachers consistently have in a world of excessive external accountability is 'covering the curriculum'. Coverage is the enemy of thought!

A culture of learning has therefore got to raise issues about the purpose and the nature of learning, and the place of both the individual and the community. This hierarchy might be usefully articulated as:

1   Learning how to become.
2   Learning how to be.
3   Learning how to do.
4   Learning how to learn.
5   Learning how to repeat.

This hierarchy suggests that learning is a complex and sophisticated process and one which is not simply concerned with the lower rungs as shown on this hierarchy. It should also be noted that learning is concerned not only with cognition, but also with emotional learning; spiritual growth; physical, social and moral development; character formation; and with the development of 'the whole person'. It should also be made clear that learning takes place throughout life, and not only in the formal 'educational' settings. Effective education will support all these ways of learning, and it will pay particular attention to the higher order aspirations of learning. The question is: to what extent does government have a concern for all stages in this hierarchy? There is much more to education than government is likely to propose.

This raises questions about what values the state legitimately might expect of schools and the education system. Among a wide range of values might be:

- peacefulness and being law abiding;
- honesty and integrity;
- enterprise and dialogue;
- creativity and imagination;
- justice and fairness;
- social inclusion and equity;
- autonomy;
- service;
- excellence.

These can be clustered and classified in many ways. They are susceptible to change and challenge, and to varying emphasis in different contexts.

Young people value ideals and adventure. They are inspired by great thoughts and dreams of the future. It would be tragic if these aspects of life and living were to be denied in an education which was restricted to the measured outcomes of education. This is to reduce education to instruction, and the person to a learner. It is to starve the spirit of its rich nourishment. Teachers should make sure that these dreams are worthy. The ways in which we teach should support this concern for the thoughts and ambitions of each person, and not deny the significance of this. This is to value the future and the personal ideals of the individual. It is to pay attention to the human values which are to be encouraged by knowing ourselves and knowing how we can use our talents in the service of others.

The debate about the purposes of education will continue in ever new contexts and in different ways. The timeless debate is one of great fascination and significance in each culture, nation and community. Deep down it will always be about helping form people and communities of humanity and hope.

Tract 9

Human scale education

Satish Kumar, born in India, is editor of Resurgence, *a journal launched in 1965 with the help of E. F. Schumacher which deals with issues concerning the future of the planet. Here he reminds us of the importance of scale in education*

Schools have become large, cumbersome and bureaucratic management structures. They resemble knowledge factories more than learning communities where students, teachers and parents know each other intimately and treat each other with respect.

We need to return to human scale of schools. Rather than being guided by external bodies such as governments and business interests, schools need to be guided by the quality of interaction between pupils, teachers, parents and local community. If a school is not rooted within a community it cannot develop a sense of belonging or become a community itself.

When the school is a community, it can organise its curriculum in a holistic and interconnected way, with teachers, pupils and parents as participants in a mutual discovery of meaning. Knowledge is not merely intellectual information; it is also an experience of relationships, with oneself, the natural world and other human beings. Such relationships go beyond academic pursuit; it includes practical and physical as much as mental, emotional and spiritual engagement. Teachers, pupils and parents work together as partners, with time for gardening, cooking, eating together, cleaning and maintaining the school and celebration of seasons, festivals and life itself. All such concepts will be alien to the system of knowledge factories where large numbers of children are crammed together. Where children are treated as empty vessels to be filled with external knowledge and information, mostly through academic means, whereas in a learning community education becomes what it is – its original meaning – to bring out – to lead out – to unfold and discover what is already there in the aptitude of the pupil.

In this holistic view of the child, he or she comes to this world with full potential. Like an acorn that has the potential to become an oak tree, each and every pupil has the potential to be him or herself; but crushed in the bureaucratic, large, knowledge factories the original and true potential is often ignored, forgotten or even suppressed. They are expected to become part of the system and if the system needs lawyers, engineers, doctors or whatever, then pupils are cajoled, forced and pressed to follow that particular career. So education is turned upside down rather than it being a voyage of self-discovery: it becomes a ladder for careerism.

So returning to scale in the context of education is to look at the schools as learning communities and not as knowledge factories.

Tract 10

Schools for life and work

Charles Handy, a Fellow of The London Business School and author of The Empty Raincoat and The Hungry Spirit, reflects on the relationship between life and work

'My education had been positively disabling.'

I left school and university with my head packed full of knowledge; enough of it, anyway, to pass all the examinations that were put in my path. It was, naturally, a rather partial sort of knowledge, containing nothing at all of the natural sciences, or of languages other than Latin and Greek, because you could not, in those days, reach the standards required of you in your chosen field, *and* be, at the same time, conversant with all the other fields of study. I was, however, considered by my teachers and my parents to be a well-educated young man.

It came as something of a shock, therefore, to encounter the world outside for the first time, and to realise that I was woefully ill-equipped, not only for the necessary business of earning a living, but, more importantly, for coping with all the new decisions which came my way, in both life and work. My first employers put it rather well: 'You have a well-trained but empty mind', they told me, 'which we will now try to fill with something useful, but don't imagine that you will be of any real value to us for the first ten years'.

A well-trained mind is not to be sneezed at, but I was soon to discover that my mind had been trained to deal with closed problems, whereas most of what I now had to deal with were open-ended problems. 'What is the cost of sales?' is a closed problem, one with a right or a wrong answer. 'What should we do about it?' is an open problem, one with any number of possible answers. Trained in analysis, I had no experience of taking decisions which might or might not turn out to be good. Knowing the right answer to a question, I came to realise, was not the same as making a difference to a situation, which was what I was supposed to be paid for.

Worse, I had been educated in an individualist culture. My scores were mine. No one else came into it, except as competitors in some imagined race. Not so in my work, I soon realised. Nothing happens there unless other people co-operate. Being an individual star would not help me much, if it was in a failing group. A group failure brought me down along with the group. Our destinies were linked, which meant that my classmates were now colleagues not competitors. Teams were something I had encountered on the sports field, not in the classroom. They were in the box marked 'fun' in my mind, not the one marked 'work'. My new challenge, I discovered, was to merge these two boxes. It was the start of my real education.

My education, I decided then, had been positively disabling. So much of the content of what I had learnt was irrelevant, while the process of learning it had cultivated a set of attitudes and behaviours which were directly opposed to what seemed to be needed in real life. I had to discard all memories of that world and start afresh.

It would be nice to think that this sort of experience could not happen now, that our schools, today, prepare people much better for life and for the work which is so crucial to a satisfactory life. But I doubt it. The subjects may appear to be a little more relevant, but we are still left to learn about work at work, and about life by living it. That will always be true, but we could, I believe, do more to make sure that the *process* of education had more in common with the processes of life and work as they are today, so that the shock of reality is less cruel. I would have more faith in a National Curriculum if it were to be more concerned with process than with content.

A school for life and work should, I suggest, subscribe to the following propositions, which apply equally to life, work and learning.

The discovery of oneself is more important than the discovery of the world

Both are important, of course, but the world will always be there. We need to build up a belief in our competence to deal with it. Too many people experience school as a failure experience. This is the worst possible starting point from which to start looking for work, particularly when so much of that work will, in future, have to be created by ourselves.

'Look for customers, not jobs', I told my own children, on leaving college, because only if you can make or do something which other people will pay you money for will you ultimately be employable. But that requires:

- self-confidence;
- a saleable skill or competence;
- social skills of quite a high order.

It is *not easy to* sell one's own goods or services. It should be a guarantee to all children, as of right, that they will have these three components of survival, by the time they leave school. If they leave without them it is the school, not they, who have failed.

We can do many things to bring it about. We can, for instance, look for ways to give every young person a success experience of some sort every year. That will be easier if the second proposition is adopted.

Everyone can be assumed to be intelligent, because intelligence comes in many forms

Three forms of intelligence are widely recognised:

- factual intelligence – the know-it-all facility that Mastermind addicts possess;
- analytic intelligence – the ability to reason and to conceptualise;
- numerate intelligence – being at ease with numbers of all sorts.

A combination of these three intelligences will get you through most tests and examinations and entitle you to be called clever.

But there are many other forms of intelligence. Howard Gardner's (1994) list of seven intelligences is but a starter and to these we can add Daniel Goleman's (1996) important concept of emotional intelligence (see boxed list). The list could continue, because there may well be other categories of intelligence.

The point is that these many and varied intelligences or abilities are all resources which we can use to contribute to the world, to earn a living and to make a difference. It cannot be proved beyond doubt, but it is a reasonable assumption that everyone has some degree of at least one of these intelligences. Nor is it obvious, looking at people in later life, that any particular set of intelligences is more important than any other. Any one of them can be developed to be the basis of a successful life and useful work.

It should be the first duty of a school for life to help the young person identify which intelligences define them, to build up an 'intelligence profile', then to encourage them to develop their best intelligences, and to work out how best to employ them in their work. This will provide the basis for that self-confidence without which little learning can occur.

Only when this has been done would it be useful to go on to try to develop the missing intelligences. A narrow focus on the first three intelligences runs the risk of labelling as stupid those who do not shine in them but who have undoubted capacities in the other areas. That is to cheat them of a life.

Further forms of intelligence

1 **Linguistic intelligence** – a facility with language and languages.
2 **Spatial intelligence** – an ability to see patterns in things.
3 **Athletic intelligence** – the skill of athletes is a recognisable form of intelligence.
4 **Intuitive intelligence** – an aptitude for sensing and seeing what is not immediately obvious.
5 **Emotional intelligence** – self-awareness and self-control, persistence, zeal and self-motivation.
6 **Practical intelligence** – often called common sense.
7 **Interpersonal intelligence** – the ability to get things done with and through others.
8 **Musical intelligence** – easy to recognise, whether in opera singers, pianists or pop groups.

Life is a marathon, not a horse-race

In a horse-race only the first three count. The rest are also-rans. In a marathon everyone who completes the course is a winner. Life is more like a marathon for most of us. We choose which races to enter, and what pace to run at, seeking, most of the time, to better ourselves. There is no winning and losing in the ultimate, only the taking part, and the getting better.

Compulsory tests at 7, 11, 14, and 16 turn education into a horse-race not a marathon, because the scores, however neutral they are intended to be, inevitably label the young person as below, or above, average. Comparative grading at set ages turns education into a sorting device, not a development process. (See Tract 22.)

The odd thing is that we have a perfectly acceptable model in our midst, one with graded examinations, high standards, but almost universal pass rates. I refer to the system of music examinations which pupils take only when their teacher estimates that they have a good chance of passing. These examinations are not age dependent – you take them at any age when you are ready for them, they set high standards and are universally respected. They are the appropriate examinations for a marathon.

Knowing 'What' is not as important as knowing 'Where', 'How' and 'Why'

Implicit in my education was the assumption that the objective of education and training was to fill my mind with as much stuff as possible, so that it would be there when I needed it. Of course, I forgot most of it. In life and in work, we learn things when we need them, not before we need them.

Knowledge, for most people, has a very short sell-by date. Unless it is used very quickly it goes off. A facility with *Words, Numbers* and *Emotions* are the real essentials. In a digital world it is crucial that we are all at ease with those numbers from an early stage, and can understand how numbers relate to each other.

Most importantly, we need to learn how to manage our emotions, in Daniel Goleman's sense of the word, to develop self-awareness, self-control and empathy and the arts of listening, resolving conflicts, and co-operation.

This, inevitably, changes the role of the learned-centred teacher. The job of the teacher is to set the task which requires the search for the knowledge, to help the individual, or the group, to seek it out, and to realise how the knowledge can be used.

School should be like work, and vice versa

Visiting a range of schools some years back, I would often start by asking how many people worked there. I always got a response in the tens, ten or 20, maybe, or 70, if it was a large school. They always left out the children in their counting.

This provoked me to think about what would happen if we treated the children as the real workers in an enlightened factory of creativity, with the teachers as the consultants and senior managers. Work would be organised around tasks to be done. Most of the work would be organised in small teams or groups. There would be competition between groups but co-operation within them. The tasks would be as real as possible, but with opportunities for skill improvement and information gathering built into the timetable.

The proposition that schools should be more like work organisations could and should be taken further. Work organisations now concentrate their own resources on their 'core task', bringing in other specialities to do what they can do better. Schools have gone down this route only to the extent of contracting out the catering and the maintenance. They could go much further, if they saw themselves, principally, as the designers and managers of a young person's development, not as the only teachers. Schools can't, and shouldn't, do everything. Practical skills such as word-processing and computing, driving, first aid, languages, home management, money management and presentation skills, could all be done, on contract, by specialist bodies, leaving the teachers free to concentrate on the more general education and development of the child.

Technical skills are best learnt, as in Germany, in the workplace, but this can be seen as an adjunct to the school and as part of education, to be monitored and arranged by the school. If the skills and attitudes needed for work are best learnt at work, then the workplace will have to get involved, not as an ultimate destination, but as part of the learning process.

A better spread of responsibilities for schooling between work and school would allow the schools to concentrate on what they do best. Fewer core staff, better paid, achieving more is the formula for productivity in industry, achieved by getting others to do what they do better and more efficiently. It is time to give the actual school a smaller but crucial role in the education of our young.

There has always been a lot of learning going on in society, but most of it has happened outside school. We ought not to regret that but to capitalise on it.

Life is a journey, which starts at school

Life, for most people, is a circular process of discovery – who we are, what we can do, and, ultimately, why we exist and what we believe. This spiralling journey is the true meaning of lifelong learning. Learning how to learn is, in its essentials, a process of discovering, and then stretching, oneself.

If we fail, this time, to leap beyond our own experience, we will fail our youth. It is indeed a time for bold imaginings, a time to bring life and work into our schools, so that our schools may more truly be part of life and work.

References

Howard Gardner, 1984, *Frames of Mind, The Theory of Multiple Intelligences*. Heinemann, London.

Daniel Goleman, 1996, *Emotional Intelligence, Why it can matter more than IQ*. Bloomsbury, London.

Tract 11

Last chance saloon for vocational education?

John Monks, Chair of the LSC Adult Learning Committee and General Secretary, European Trade Union Confederation, reflects on reforming the 14–19 curriculum

The phrase *'ladder of opportunity for all young people'* has been bandied about a lot by Government Ministers recently as they justify yet another phase of schooling reform. The latest 'hard sell' for reform is focused on the schooling system experienced by teenagers as set out in the White Paper, *14–19: Opportunity and Excellence.*

One of the key objectives of the 14–19 reform agenda is to raise the status of vocational education in schools so that it has parity of esteem with the academic route. However, according to one estimate, this is the eighth time in the past 25 years that UK governments have pledged to achieve this end.

Nevertheless, in spite of understandable scepticism, there is an air of cautious optimism around that maybe, just maybe, they might pull it off this time. *Well, who cares?* may be your response if you are a teacher, parent, or teenager whose overriding concern is with achieving a university place. And in one sense this sentiment echoes one successful element of Government policy over the past two decades – the rapid increase in the proportion of our young people progressing to higher education.

However, as the 14–19 White Paper highlights, our schooling system continues to be blighted by major failings. First and foremost, too many young people continue to leave education at too early an age and completely ill-equipped for the modern world of work. In addition, unlike most of our European neighbours, we continue to conspire to label young people who do not progress to university as failures and we treat vocational career pathways with a degree of national disdain.

Fortunately, the development of Modern Apprenticeships and Foundation degrees does provide new high-quality vocational routes for young people and the 14–19 White Paper sets out a convincing plan vastly to improve the 'vocational offer' in schools.

What will this mean for UK schools in the coming years? Well, one measure of success will be if our secondary schools genuinely evolve into institutions where academic and vocational studies are integrated and equally respected and all pupils experience both educational worlds. If this is achieved there is a strong possibility that our schools will become ladders of opportunity for all our young people in the future.

Tract 12

Learning families

Titus Alexander, Editor, examines the role of families in learning

'It takes a village to educate a child'

(African proverb)

Families are our most formative and important places of learning. Children spend less than 15% of waking time in school between birth and 16. Parents and carers are responsible for children three-quarters of waking time. Children spend much of this time with child-minders, television, other children, nursery and many different people. But parents have a major responsibility for how this time is used. This is the time, particularly in the early years, when children are learning how to speak, think, act and learn for themselves.

The influence of good parenting at home is much greater than differences in the quality of schools at primary level. At 16 parental involvement still has a significant effect but school has more influence on achievement and adjustment (Desforges 2003).[1] Parental involvement in a child's schooling between age 7 and 16 also has more influence on attainment than family background, size and parents' own educational level (Feinstein and Symons 1999),[2] although the extent and form of parental involvement is strongly influenced by family social class.

Educational failure is strongly associated with lack of parental interest. Harsh, inconsistent or abusive parenting is also linked to low attainment, anti-social behaviour and mental illness in adult life. The relatively small proportion of children who have most difficulty at school, are most disruptive in class and behave badly are much more likely to lack parental support. They are also more likely to have a difficult life, commit crime and suffer from alcoholism or drug abuse. By age 28 the additional cost to society of children with persistent anti-social behaviour at age 10 is many times greater than those with no problems, about £70,000 at 1998 prices (Scott *et al.* 2001).[3]

How we educate our children therefore needs to involve parents as educators and families as places of learning. We expect too much from teachers and schools to make up for parental support where it is lacking and we fail to give parents the support which would enable them to succeed. This is not helped by allowing some schools to select only the most able children (and parents), since this dumps the difficulties on others. But we cannot expect schools to cope with all children and parents, however challenging, unless we radically change the nature and role of schools.

If we want all children to achieve their full potential, we need to treat every parent as the most enduring educator of their child. Instead of seeing the school or nursery as the place where children go to learn (and parents help out), we need to recognise the home and community as the *primary* place of learning for every child. The job of schools, nurseries, libraries and other places of learning is to extend, deepen and support learning that is rooted in the home.

'Home' means many different things for different children. For most it is a safe, secure loving household with one or two parents. For many, home has a different language, culture or ethos from school, including different dialects and cultures among native English speakers. For some, home is shared between two parents and families in different households, or between an extended family that embraces communities thousands of miles away. For about one in ten, home is a difficult, frightening, sometime violent place. For a few it is a series of carers and institutions, temporary housing and constant insecurity. As a society, and as schools, we need to include the whole range of homes and families in our thinking, because we are all connected and each part affects the whole in some way.

The Government has begun to recognise the importance of parents as educators, through Sure Start, funding for family learning, the extended schools programme, and many other measures. The 2003 Green Paper *Every Child Matters* (DfES 2003)[4] aims to strengthen support for parents and families further.

But it is local people, community groups, schools and councils that will actually make the difference. The emerging national and local framework for family learning and support makes it possible that we can begin to give every child a good start in life, but it can only happen if adults give every single child the love, encouragement, respect and inspiration to flourish as a human being.

What can schools do?

In their present form, schools are highly specialised institutions designed to manage and instruct groups of children for fixed periods of time. Almost all their efforts and resources are focused on the relatively small amount of waking time children spend in school. But how well children learn in the classroom also depends on what happens in the rest of their lives. The results on which schools are measured – children's achievement in a few subjects – depend on many factors outside their control.

Schools rely on parents, carers and the community to ensure that children have a certain level of behaviour, language and other essential skills before they can begin to do their job properly. They rely on parents to encourage learning at school and to support learning outside school. And they assume parents to lead relatively stable lives: living at the same place, able to provide for their children, and not so stressed, depressed or aggressive that their children have difficulty coping.

Many schools support parents and provide additional help for children who have difficulties at home. They treat parents as partners in their child's education and involve other agencies to provide additional support. But almost all schools are still trying to get parents and children to fit round the school as an institution. Very few have really begun to put the needs of children and parents at the centre of learning. The real transformation will come when schools stop trying to manage batches of children according to a prescribed national plan and start responding to the needs of particular people – children, carers and parents – who make up their community.

Schools cannot make *any* assumptions about children's home background. Children from very poor, deprived backgrounds may have one parent absolutely committed to her children's learning, providing books, extra tuition and constant encouragement. Affluent parents may shower their kids with things as a substitute for love, but provide no support or intellectual stimulation. Parents may not be able to speak English, but have a network of support that fosters constant opportunities for learning. Parents may be angry and hostile to the school, but fiercely protective and supportive of their child. The permutations are endless.

To put the needs of children and parents at the centre of learning, all schools need to:

- create relationships of mutual respect and honesty with children, parents, carers and families;
- enable parents and the people who work with them to really understand the importance of parents as educators and what that means in practice;
- ensure that parents have the information and support they need, for parenting as well as learning.

How schools do this depends on the age range of children; the parents and communities who use the school; and the resources available. But there are seven strategic questions that can help almost any school to encourage learning families.

Strategic questions for schools

1 How do you create a constructive relationship with every child and family?
   The first impression and first contact can shape a person's perception for
   life, so make this a magical moment. Home visiting; listening to parents'
   hopes and fears; being honest about the school's strengths, weaknesses
   and aspirations; involving current parents in supporting new parents are
   a few of the many ways schools use to do this. Address concerns early,
   frankly and empathetically.

2 How do you tell parents what you are doing and why?
   Clear and accessible information is fundamental, about what children are
   learning and how parents can help; about policies, resources and responsibilities; about the importance of parents. Word of mouth is best for the
   most important things, with written material for reference.

3 How do you give feedback to children and parents on how the child is
   doing and what she needs?
   We all need clear, specific and actionable information to learn: regular
   useful information, through a home-learning journal, telephone, email or
   personal conversation can be more useful than the termly report and
   'parents' evening'.

4 How do you create a community among parents and involve them in the
   life of the school?
   A regular 'class meeting' of all parents in each class or form, once a term,
   can create a forum for discussion and a focus for a deeper relationship
   among parents.

5 How do you involve parents in making policies and decisions?
   The 'class meetings' of all parents can raise concerns, propose initiatives,
   discuss policies or elect representatives to a Parents' Council.

6 How do you open wider opportunities for all parents?
   Work with other agencies to offer information and support for parenting
   and learning beyond school, including activities, courses, work and other
   opportunities to enrich life for all.

7 How do you make the most of life's transitions?
   Starting school can be uplifting or traumatic. Many children lose a year
   of learning moving between primary and secondary. Transitions from
   infancy to childhood to adolescence to adulthood are significant processes
   in which parents and schools lay the framework for learning and life.
   Systematically asking parents and young people to evaluate their time
   in school can provide invaluable information about how to improve
   school for all.

These seven questions can help to develop a whole-school commitment to
learning with parents and transform schools into community centres for lifelong learning.

Notes

1   *The Impact of Parental Involvement, Parental Support and Family Education on Pupil Achievement and Adjustment: A Literature Review*, by Professor Charles Desforges, Emeritus Professor, University of Exeter, and Dr Leon Feinstein, London School of Economics, which can be downloaded, free, from www.dfes.gov.uk
2   Feinstein, L. and Symons, J., 1999, *Attainment in Secondary School*, Oxford Economic Papers, 51.
3   Scott, S., Knapp, M., Henderson, J. and Maughan, B., 2001, Financial consequences of social exclusion: follow-up study of antisocial children into adulthood, *BMJ*, 323: 191, 28 July.
4   DfES, 2003, CM 5860, web: http://www.dfes.gov.uk/everychildmatters/

Tract 13

Seize the day, baby boomers!

Elizabeth Allen is the headteacher of Newstead Wood School for Girls. She writes here as an experienced leader in secondary schools of many kinds and offers a challenge to her 'baby boomer' colleagues

Thank goodness we are changing our squash racquets for binoculars, our designer trainers for stout walking shoes. The baby boomers have come of age: we have stopped dashing around, making ourselves agile and competitive. All the educational indulgences lavished on the post-war generation have paid off. And now, we are reflective, experienced, well-read and, most of all, a confident bunch of school leaders. We came into the job, in the 1960s, to change the world and we are on the brink of doing so. If we keep our nerve, we might just bring off the biggest and best bloodless revolution in schools: if we lose our nerve in the face of some niggly legislation, budget worries or sheer age fatigue, then the best chance to get achievement for all will slip away. So, come on, you fellow post-war babies, let's 'Seize the Day' and the education agenda.

Our education, whatever its faults, was founded on the high aspirations of the 1944 Education Act that wanted to 'Build a Better Britain'. When we first started the school leaders of the day made us think about the impact of nurture and environment on a child's capacity to know and understand. Not all of us put the theory into practice: it was a hit-and-miss affair, dependent on the school and the headteacher we had found. If the school was a 'hit', a young teacher in the 1970s could experiment, with School Council Humanities projects, Nuffield Science and many innovative approaches to school organisation and curriculum. If the school was a 'miss', a young teacher could either conduct exciting educational experiments unnoticed by a dormant head or get bogged down in uninspired, uninspiring crowd control. The best of today's school leaders probably experienced both.

Although the schools of the 1970s allowed leaders of the future to rise to the surface in middle management, the lack of accountability and inequality of opportunity in the system for children and for teachers remained intolerable. But the baby boomers were not experienced enough in school leadership to grasp the opportunities and so once more legislation was used in the hope of achieving equity through comprehensive schools. We learned much from the comprehensive movement, chiefly to acknowledge the impact of contextual factors on learning outcomes. However, a decade later, we still were not confident enough to grab the National Curriculum agenda. Here comes the biggest 'if only': in 1982 Her Majesty's Inspectors proposed our ideal National Curriculum, but what we got instead was the 1988 Education Reform Act. It has taken us 15 years to regain our confidence sufficiently to wrestle its version of the National Curriculum into submission.

Ironically, it has been successive governments' drives for school accountability that has led to our confidence, our 'coming of age' as school leaders and our readiness for autonomy. Ofsted and league tables were vital in ensuring equality of opportunity and in raising standards. As well as having a clear vision and mission for their children, schools *should* have service level agreements with their funders – government, local authority and ratepayers – and be, literally, accountable.

Schools need to be led by confident, intuitive leaders who are ahead of the DfES agenda. These are people who:

- have always accelerated learning for the bright;
- know that thinking skills, communication and life skills underpin the curriculum and the organisation;
- have community development and citizenship at the heart of their mission;
- see young people as individuals on a personal journey to achievement, when their learning needs are met;
- are equally committed to the personal and professional development of their staff – all of them;
- celebrate the achievements of all, including the most able;
- are crusaders for inclusion.

Confidence is high amongst school leaders. With the right balance of support and accountability from our stakeholders, the current generation of school leaders will bring about the most positive, radical development in education for 60 years – our lifetime!

Government: Can trust us. We have proved our commitment to achievement for all young people. Most schools are self-managing, setting rigorous targets. So, no more annual knee-jerk legislation; light touch Ofsted, please and replace Performance Tables with schools' aggregated targets. And decide: collaboration or competition? The muddle between the two is madness. And listen to Mike Tomlinson, because we think he may be right.

Local Authorities: Can use school expertise. All the consultants and advisers you need are in your schools.

Teachers: Can focus on the real business – how young people learn best. They must educate their own emotional and spiritual intelligences so that they can be sensitive to their students' needs and abilities.

School Leaders: We have control. In our hands, schools have never been better. Autonomy and diversity are of our making and young people 'have never had it so good'.

School leadership has come of age. It is no coincidence that both the General Teaching Council and the National College of School Leadership have come about as we reach our prime. Of course, there have always been great school leaders but never in this number and never so collectively articulate. We are confident in our abilities to empower the young people in our school. We are very capable of engendering and embedding developments of massive proportions when they are right for our children. Look at Literacy, Numeracy, Specialist Schools, Arts/Sportsmark, IIP, Chartered Schools, Beacon, Leading Edge Partnerships, major restructuring to the curriculum and to the public examination system and e-learning. From TVEI onwards, the baby boom generation of school leaders has led and managed change far beyond what we envisaged in the late 1960s. We are having our day. And our pupils will have the skills for their lifetime.

AGENDA FOR CHANGE

'Children learn as much from the way we treat them as from any particular set of lessons in class.'

We value our children when we:

1   educate them for their future rather than our past;
2   treat them as fellow humans with the capacity to achieve great things;
3   have a vision for their future.

We nourish our children when we make it possible for them to:

4   enjoy and protect a sustainable plant;
5   show love, care and compassion;
6   appreciate and create beauty;
7   have the urge and the abilities to serve others;
8   care about justice and fairness;
9   learn through human scale experiences.

We educate our children when we enable them to:

10   become;
11   be;
12   do;
13   learn; and
14   repeat.

Our schools best help our children when they know that:

15   the discovery of oneself is more important than the discovery of the world;
16   everyone can be assumed to be intelligent, because intelligence comes in many forms;
17   life is a marathon where everyone wins, not a race where only the first three count;
18   knowing 'What' is not as important as knowing 'Where', 'How' and 'Why';
19   school should be like work, and vice versa.

Chapter 3

School matters: Learning matters

Letter to a school governor

Dear Governor,

School matters: Learning matters

You have one of the most important political jobs in the country. I say political, because the buck stops with you, the governors. You are responsible for the achievements, policies, staff and finance of the school. The head is responsible for day-to-day leadership and management. But you appoint her and decide the strategy within which she works. You may delegate most decisions to the head – and often that is the best thing to do – but you are responsible for the results. Teachers lead when it comes to learning, but you are responsible for selecting and supporting them, and for the surrounding ethos which sustains the quality of learning. You may defer to school traditions, government policies or external advisers – and they bring accumulated knowledge which cannot be ignored – but you decide what happens. Ultimately you set the school's direction, standards and values. You must reconcile conflicting pressures one way or other. You decide what happens in a crisis. You carry the can.

As a governor, you are often left out of national discussions about education, or only mentioned in passing. Government guidelines describe your duties and responsibilities in great detail. Ministers praise the 'key role' you play in 'helping your school provide the best possible education for all its pupils', by which they mean 'supporting the head and staff'. But when it comes to new initiatives, you are often by-passed or treated as a transmission mechanism for adapting national policies to your school.

This seriously under-estimates your potential as the grassroots government of education. In many ways your job is more important than a backbench Member of Parliament or local councillor. They may represent thousands of people. You have a direct responsibility for the achievements and life-chances of each child who attends your school. MPs and councillors are involved in many issues, but you have a specific responsibility for each young person enrolled at your school. The people you appoint, the resources you allocate, the policies you carry out and the example you set have a direct influence on their lives. Your decisions directly affect their opportunities for learning now. Few backbench MPs or councillors have that kind of direct responsibility for a specific group of people.

We explore the implications of this in the next tract.

Titus Alexander and John Potter

The importance of governors governing

Titus Alexander, Editor, explores the reasons why governors have such a critical role to play in transforming schools for the future

How schools are run makes a big difference to pupils' lives. Ground-breaking studies of secondary and junior schools by Michael Rutter, Peter Mortimore and their colleagues in *Fifteen Thousand Hours* and *School Matters: the Junior Years*, identified 10 to 12 essential elements of effective schools. They show 'conclusively, that whether a child attends one school or another – regardless of natural talents and family background – it is likely to make a major difference to how much progress the child makes'. Since then there has been a lot more research on school effectiveness, highlighting the importance of factors such as school intake, location, resources, staff and its particular history. Nevertheless, the overwhelming evidence from many studies of schools in different settings is that these 10 to 12 elements are the keys to a good school.

Of course, governors are not alone in influencing learning at their school. Parents and families are by far the biggest influence on children's achievement. But how the school involves parents in their children's learning is largely down to the governors and the way they work with staff, parents and other stakeholders. Children's behaviour and peer pressure make a huge difference to learning. But how the school fosters friendship, deals with conflict and creates a culture of co-operation is your responsibility. The local authority and government decide the general level of finance, but you decide how it is spent, whether to raise funds from other sources or to campaign for more money. Although the Government lays down broad policies for curriculum and management, you decide how to respond to them.

Governing a school is like governing a city or a state, as Charles Handy points out in his book, *Understanding Schools as Organizations* (1990). In some ways it is simpler, because the purpose is much clearer. But this also makes it more difficult. Because so much seems to have been decided already, governors often feel that they only rubber-stamp decisions made elsewhere or respond to crises, many of which have been created elsewhere as well.

A school governor may have less power than national governments or the Council, but neither Whitehall nor the Town Hall can run your school. Still less can they inspire and support its staff, students and parents to be the best they can possibly be. This is the real source of your power.

Your responsibilities for education

Governors are collectively 'responsible for promoting high standards of educational achievement' and for how the school is run. But this raises important questions about what governors interpret as 'high standards of educational achievement' and how to promote them. Are high standards of educational achievement the same as exam results? Some commentators, like former Chief Inspector Chris Woodhead, challenge the standards measured by exams today and accuse the education establishment of colluding with cheating by students and 'grade inflation' by examiners so that exams are less demanding and the results unreliable. In which case, should you, as governors, shop around for better exams? Or should governors join Chris Woodhead's 'class war' for traditional standards and campaign to remove the shackles of the state from schools?

Are standards mainly about achieving 'skills for life and work', the aims of the Department for Education and Skills? In which case, do governors accept the Government's view of what these are, as set out in the national strategies for literacy, numeracy, the National Curriculum and the rest? Or should a school concentrate on teaching skills which get young people into the best-paid jobs the market offers, which may be in the arts, sports or finance rather than academic subjects? Or does it mean life skills for personal development, relationships, managing money and coping with modern life?

Should governors have a more diverse, holistic view of educational achievement, which includes creativity, citizenship, emotional development, physical education and other non-academic activities? In which case, how do you decide what they are, how do you promote them, and how do you know if they are being achieved?

The three viewpoints summarise the choice between three distinct approaches to education summarised in the letter to readers at the start – **Traditionalist, Functionalist** and **Holist**. These are not political parties, but they represent clear policy choices for your school. The staff you appoint, the policies you adopt, the way you relate to parents or respond to Government initiatives, will all depend on how much you follow one or other of these broad approaches. You can mix'n'match aspects from each approach – and each approach has its virtues – but the choice is yours to make.

Each approach expresses a different vision of society. They are unavoidably political choices. Governing a school is not about carrying out decisions made on high. It is about making choices which shape the lives of all who belong to the school community, choices which can transform the place they live for generations.

All the tracts in the following section are broadly within the 'holistic' approach to education. They provide food for thought, discussion and action by governing bodies.

Tract 15

Starting with learners

We set the scene from the following tracts with a brief excerpt from the Association of Teachers and Lecturers (ATL) minimum requirements for effective learning

'As a minimum, learners also need to be able to:

- ask their own questions;
- think critically and creatively;
- reason effectively;
- motivate themselves and others;
- work with others;
- make choices;
- manage, monitor and improve their own learning to solve problems.'

Tract 16

Creating a learning to learn school

Toby Greany, Policy and Information Director, Campaign for Learning, and Bill Lucas, Independent Consultant describe fresh approaches to learning that are already proving effective and replicable

I welcome *Creating a learning to learn school* for the evidence it provides of the impact of Learning to Learn approaches on raising standards, pupil motivation and teacher morale. All three are top priorities for this Government. I also welcome the challenge it provides to make stronger links between schooling and lifelong learning.

(David Miliband, Minister of State for
School Standards, DfES)[1]

The Campaign for Learning's ground-breaking *Learning to Learn in Schools* action-research project explores what happens when you teach pupils how they learn.[2] It also outlines new thinking on what a learning to learn approach might actually look like in schools.

'Learning to learn' and why it matters

Since we cannot know what knowledge will be most needed in the future, it is senseless to try to teach it in advance. Instead, we should try to turn out people who love learning so much and learn so well that they will be able to learn whatever needs to be learned.

(John Holt)

'Learning to learn' is a process of discovery about learning. It involves a set of principles and skills which, if understood and used, help learners learn more effectively and so become learners for life. At its heart is the belief that learning is learnable.

In brief, 'learning to learn' offers pupils an awareness of how they prefer to learn and their learning strengths; how they can motivate themselves and have the self-confidence to succeed; things they should consider, such as the importance of water, nutrition, sleep and a positive environment for learning; some of the specific strategies they can use, for example to improve their memory or make sense of complex information; and some of the habits they should develop, such as reflecting on their learning so as to improve next time.

This approach to 'learning to learn' draws on, and is indebted to, a wealth of thinking and practice from a range of different disciplines. These include cognitive psychology, neuroscience, Formative Assessment/ Assessment for Learning, Thinking Skills, Accelerated Learning, Emotional Intelligence, and work on learning environments, health and nutrition for learning. Some of these influences have emerged from academic research, others from teachers in schools simply establishing what works or what feels right.

Why is learning to learn important?

Lifelong learning is a 'must have' for both individuals and UK plc. More than ever before pupils leaving school today will need to continue learning throughout their lives and that those who don't will be at the greatest risk of social exclusion. The pitiful basic skills of the UK's prison population (60% are functionally illiterate and innumerate) is just one piece of evidence that backs up this assertion. Our belief, which we are exploring through the Learning to Learn research project, is that pupils who understand themselves better as learners and know how to improve their own learning will be more likely to continue learning throughout life and so avoid that social exclusion.

So what actually makes a good learner? Or, put another way, what knowledge, skills and attitudes/attributes should a 'learning to learn' approach develop? In answer to these questions the Campaign has developed the 5 Rs for lifelong learning model set out on these pages, gratefully acknowledging the work of both Guy Claxton and Alistair Smith on which it is based.

By using a range of approaches to develop the 5 Rs, schools can achieve their core purpose, namely preparing all young people so that they can, and do, continue learning effectively throughout their lives.

The 'learning to learn' research project

The key question underpinning the learning to learn research was: *how can pupils be enabled to learn most effectively so that each one has the best chance to achieve his or her full potential?*

Twenty-five schools took part in the first year of the research. A broadly representative range of schools was selected, including schools in the bottom 5% for Key Stage 1 results, where approximately one-third of pupils are on the Special Needs Register, where one-third of pupils have an ethnic minority background and where significant numbers of pupils entered the school with a reading age below their chronological age.

> My priorities as a Head are to enable the school to be in control of its teaching and learning environment; to promote a culture of professionalism and debate; to empower staff and children; to raise the self-esteem of pupils and to create learners who will take on the world (or feel they can).
>
> (Neil Baker, Headteacher, Christ Church Primary School, Wiltshire)

There were 16 secondary schools and nine primary schools, four of which focused on nursery and reception pupils. Two schools were in Wales and the remainder were spread throughout England. Each school involved teams of teachers in implementing the research, although the size of these varied from single departments to all staff. Staff attended termly professional development and three residential events run by the Campaign and also received visits and ongoing telephone and email support.

Each school developed its own research hypotheses and evaluation approaches in consultation with Dr Rodd, the independent research consultant. The staff involved collected quantitative and qualitative data on the impact of their approach. Each school was, subsequently, required to produce a short report outlining their findings at the end of each phase.

How schools have introduced learning to learn

The five Rs for lifelong learning provided a basis for each approach. Every learner must develop a capacity for readiness, resourcefulness, resilience, remembering and reflectiveness. Each of the five terms refers to something that the pupils learn *how to do*.

1. Readiness Pupils know how:	2. Resourcefulness Pupils know how:	3. Resilience Pupils know how:	4. Remembering Pupils know how:
• to assess own motivation • to set goals and connect to the learning to achieve a positive learning state, including their preferred learning environment.	• the mind works and how humans learn • to assess their own preferred learning style, including how to take in information • to seek out and use information, including through ICT to communicate effectively in different ways	• to apply learned optimism and self-efficacy approaches • to empathise and use EQ approaches • to proceed when stuck to ask (critical) questions.	• to use different memory approaches • to make connections • to apply learning, including in different contexts.

5. Reflectiveness
Pupils know how: to ask questions, observe, see patterns, experiment and evaluate learning.

The different approaches

The schools adopted different approaches to the developing learning to learn strategies.

Stand alone learning to learn courses

These included learning to learn induction courses or ongoing timetabled lessons for pupils to explore how people learn and how they could learn to learn. The content of these courses varied but all focused on developing some or all aspects of the five Rs for lifelong learning.

Using models of learning

Different models of learning were explored through different approaches to planning and giving lessons. These were designed to help pupils develop their own models of learning.

Developing self-esteem, confidence and motivation

Some schools assessed different approaches to developing readiness, self-esteem, confidence and motivation through strategies such as Assessment for Learning, Accelerated Learning, Gestalt theory, peer teaching and Neuro-Linguistic Programming (NLP).

Learning styles

A number of schools monitored the emergence of preferred learning styles and/or helped pupils identify their preferred learning style and the impact on independent learning.

Multiple intelligences and emotional intelligence

Multiple intelligences approaches were used to help raise standards and develop learning capacity. Some schools also explored how emotional intelligence could be developed, for example through the Circle Time approach pioneered by Jenny Mosely (see Tract 18).

Learning to learn approaches embedded in specific curriculum areas

Some educators explored the application of thinking skills and learning to learn approaches in specific subject areas, such as Thinking Through Geography.

Learning to learn approaches with specific groups of pupils

One school identified specific target and control groups of gifted and talented pupils and monitored the effect of applying learning to learn approaches. Another school assessed the impact of providing intensive mentoring support for disaffected pupils by mentors trained in NLP/learning to learn approaches. Several schools assessed the differential impact of learning to learn on boys and girls.

Pupils' learning strategies

Some educators developed pupils' resourcefulness through providing students with a toolkit of learning to learn techniques, such as mind-mapping techniques and NLP.

Teaching and learning approaches

Many evaluated the effectiveness of different teaching strategies such as delivering information through visual, auditory and kinaesthetic approaches, following a learning cycle in all planning frameworks and/or teaching to meet the needs of different intelligences.

Exploring other factors that affect learning

The schools also paid attention to other factors that were likely to affect the quality of learning. Some explored the impact of different aspects of a learning-friendly *environment* such as creating low threat, high challenge learning opportunities, the use of ICT, interactive whiteboards and music in different curriculum areas, and the use of posters with learning messages and other visual stimulii as part of classroom display.

Other schools explored the impact of giving pupils information about how *nutrition, water* and *sleep* affect learning and/or provided brain-friendly food in school and access to water in the classroom. Others looked at the impact of brain gym, yoga, meditation and relaxation techniques on learning and exam results. One school explored the impact of an American football course on motivation and concentration among disaffected boys.

Some schools explored the impact of different learning to learn approaches on *memory and recall* and how this affected exam success. Most schools used different approaches to develop pupils' ability to reflect on and improve learning.

Most schools also assessed the impact of *engaging other staff* in supporting learning to learn approaches for example, through professional development and the production of resources/staff handbooks, etc. Some schools explored how pupils could be helped to transfer and apply learning to learn approaches to different contexts.

Some schools assessed the impact of running courses, holding information evenings and producing resources for *parents* about learning to learn, including the impact on parental perceptions of the school.

Many of the schools investigated aspects of developing a wider school culture to support learning to learn, for example through changes to the School Development Plan, curriculum, use of assemblies, citizenship learning, out of school hours learning, etc.

The benefits of introducing 'learning to learn': the research findings

Overall, the first two years of the project demonstrated that 'learning to learn' approaches can help:

- raise standards;
- improve teacher morale; and
- increase pupil motivation.

There are positive effects on standards of achievement by pupils and the motivation of pupils, teachers and parents who understand and develop their preferred learning styles.

The learner

> The most important thing I learned this year is that there are lots of different ways of learning.
>
> (Pupil)

Students of all ages are more positive about learning and motivated to learn when they understand their preferred learning styles and intelligences. Encouraging the development of pupils' learning dispositions, including the 5 Rs for lifelong learning, enhances pupils' perceptions of themselves as learners and improves attainment levels. Pupils learn best when teachers present information in a range of ways to meet the different learning styles in their classrooms. Pupils learn best when they enjoy themselves or have fun, indicating that their emotional state is fundamental to learning.

The learning process

As learners enjoy experiences of brain-friendly, student-centred learning – including the importance of self-esteem and motivation in learning – they notice positive effects on their motivation, independence and standards of work. Foundation Stage and Key Stage 1 and 2 pupils demonstrate increased enjoyment of and improved learning when they understand how they learn best and have a range of learning tools to apply to different tasks. Learning to learn courses help primary and secondary students identify and apply a range of strategies which they think help them learn at school and at home.

The vast majority of secondary students enjoy and value taking part in learning to learn sessions and courses. They think learning to learn courses are worthwhile, that what they learn helps with other schoolwork and that they should be part of the regular school timetable.

The learning environment

Improving the physical environment of learning has positive benefits. Factors identified include the use of displays, pictures and music, the use of resources including ICT and interactive whiteboards, and where pupil groupings are taken into consideration in planning for learning. Attractive physical learning environments are associated with improved pupil attitudes, behaviour and performance. Posters, pictures and displays provide pupils with a structure through which to recognise, select and reinforce learning behaviours. The use of music as a tool for learning improves standards and motivation in secondary students.

The teacher–learning facilitator

> Learning to learn has transformed the way I teach and the way I think about teaching and learning.
>
> (Teacher)

Learning to learn has enormous benefits for teacher motivation, continuing professional development, interaction with other adults in the classroom (such as parents and teaching assistants) and for mentoring both pupils and colleagues. Improved pupil performance in examinations is associated with teachers who actively think about pedagogy. Most teachers found that student learning and behaviour improved and their own professional motivation and enjoyment increased when they employed learning to learn approaches.

Parents

> It offers better all-round education in a non-regimented fashion. It serves to improve my child's life chances.
>
> (Parent)

Parents who participate in a learning to learn course become more effective in supporting their children's learning and become better learners themselves. Parents who understand about learning to learn approaches feel more confident about trying different ways to help their children learn at home.

The body

Pupils learn better if they have free access to drinking water. Exercise in the forms of brain gym and sport has a positive effect on pupil enjoyment of and motivation for learning. The use of music in classrooms has a positive effect on calming and relaxing pupils. Engaging in specific de-stressing activities before writing in examinations improves examination results.

The next phase

> Creating a Learning to Learn School is far more than a teachers' tool-kit. It has the potential to make us all more self-aware as learners and challenges us to broaden and deepen our repertoire of learning strategies.
>
> (Heather Du Quesnay, Director and Chief Executive, National College for School Leadership)

The Campaign for Learning is now co-ordinating a larger research project (phase three) which will build on and develop the findings to date, working with clusters of up to 12 schools in Cheshire, Enfield and Cornwall.

See www.campaign-for-learning.org.uk for more details.

Notes

1   *Source*: Foreword to *Creating a 'learning to learn' school: research and practice for raising standards, motivation and morale*, Toby Greany and Jill Rodd, Network Educational Press, 2003.
2   The thinking and research findings summarised in this article are based on the two project reports *Teaching pupils how to learn*, CfL/NEP, 2002; and *Creating a learning to learn school*, CfL/NEP, 2003.

Tract 17

The habit of freedom

Anita Roddick, Founder of The Body Shop, reflects on the importance of the habit of freedom in education

Let's help our children to develop the habit of freedom. To encourage them to celebrate who and what they are.

Let's stop teaching children to fear change and protect the status quo. Let's teach them to enquire and debate. To ask questions until they hear answers. And the way to do it is to change the way of traditional schooling.

Our educational system does its best to ignore and suppress the creative spirit of children. It teaches them to listen unquestioningly to authority. It insists that education is just knowledge contained in subjects and the purpose of education is to get a job. What's left out is sensitivity to others, non-violent behaviour, respect, intuition, imagination and a sense of awe and wonderment.

If we develop a moral sensitivity of caring rather than coercion then maybe the practice that has led to child labour in their millions, that allows armies to turn kids into killers, and a society where child prostitution is one of its fastest growing industries will stop.

Tract 18

Self-esteem and motivation

Jenny [Mosely], the pioneer of Quality Circle Time, explores strategies and tactics to address self-esteem and motivation among children and young people

In 1987, a task force was set up by the California State Department to investigate the underlying causes of the social problems that beset American society. In its final report, it stated that their researches led to the conviction that *'the lack of self-esteem is central to most of the personal and social ills plaguing our state and nation'* (1990: 40). If self-esteem enhancement is important to society as a whole then it is even more vital within the education system, for it is there that we have a powerful opportunity to influence children's potential to become secure and productive adults.

Each of us has a view of our mental and physical characteristics and an opinion about our comparative worth that is called our self-concept. We begin to develop this concept at a very early age through the way that we are treated and spoken to by others, initially our parents or primary care-givers. Subsequently we learn much about ourselves from interaction with *significant others* in the world around us, which in our society usually means teachers and peers (Lawrence 1996). Our self-concept defines our beliefs about our place in the world, modifies our attitudes and drives our behaviour. It is, however, dynamic and capable of change. We review it constantly as we grow and develop and shape and reshape it in the social situations that we encounter (Wetherall and Maybin 1996).

Self-concept is an umbrella term for the range of ideas that we hold about ourselves and can be split into three major components. We have a self-image, which is the person that we think we are and an image of who we wish to be (our ideal or desired self). At the border between these two images is the part of ourselves that sits in judgement and measures our perception of our worth in the world. This is called our self-esteem. People who see themselves as valuable and worthy are said to have high self-esteem, and those who look at themselves and find little of value are said to have low self-esteem.

People with high self-esteem have confidence in their skills and competence and enjoy facing the challenges that life offers them. They willingly work in teams because they are sure of themselves and enjoy taking the opportunity to contribute. People who feel good about themselves are motivated to increase their self-esteem and seek personal growth, development, and improvement by exercising their capabilities. Such people benefit from social interaction, but those of us who have low self-esteem tend to feel awkward, shy, conspicuous, and unable to express themselves. They worry about making a mistake, being embarrassed or exposing themselves to ridicule. Often they compound their problems by opting for avoidance strategies because they hold the belief that whatever they do will result in failure and further demoralisation. Conversely, they may compensate for their lack of self-esteem by exhibiting boastful and arrogant behaviour to 'cover up' their sense of unworthiness. Their tendency to look for evidence of inadequacy immobilises them and they are resistant to change because they view it as threatening and risky. Accepting positive feedback is often viewed as far more risky than accepting negative feedback. Furthermore, such individuals have problems with locus of control – while high self-esteem children will attribute their success to internal characteristics; those with low self-esteem will account for their successes by finding reasons that are outside of themselves. ('I got lucky, my teacher helped me.') As a result, they never attain awareness of their personal potential and are unable to discover the extent of their capabilities (Burns 1982).

The desire for self-enhancement is the motivating force behind the need to achieve (Owens *et al.* 2001) but, as is explained above, for children with low levels of self-esteem, success is an intrinsically threatening experience. This inter-relationship between levels of self-esteem and motivation has many implications for teachers who need to recognise the problems that some children face as they strive for self-enhancement. It is vital that schools institute intervention programmes designed to tackle signs of low self-esteem if they are to ensure that all children achieve the success of which they are capable.

The social nature of self-esteem acquisition suggests that group activities may be particularly beneficial for enhancing self-esteem because such activities enable pupils to experience positive feedback from peers as well as from adults.

The Quality Circle Time Model is specifically designed to offer children a means of reassessing their self-concept and, thereby, gives them an opportunity to raise their self-esteem, which will then galvanise their motivation and improve their chance of achieving academic success.

Quality Circle Time practitioners believe that the school community as a whole has a responsibility to provide the adults in a school with opportunities for self-enhancement if they are to provide children with an ethos that is favourable to raising children's self-esteem. This puts listening at the centre of the school timetable.

Quality Circle Time sets up systems within which adults and children can speak with themselves and each other. These are:

- **Circle Time** provides children with an opportunity to experience positive relationships with other people. For children, games and exercises are designed to foster a sense of the class as a community, and to establish a safe boundary within which other activities can take place. For adults, circle meetings are designed to discuss issues and to celebrate success.
- **Bubble Time and Talk Time** are one-to-one listening systems, respectively for primary schools and for secondary schools but can be adapted for nursery children.
- **Think Books** are offered as a daily non-verbal communication system for older children.

Quality Circle Time provide the ideal group listening system for enhancing self-esteem, promoting moral values, building a sense of team and developing social skills. It is a democratic system that gives equal rights and opportunities. It offers a practical opportunity to discuss concerns, consider and debate moral values, practise positive behaviours and work out solutions and action plans in an enjoyable context which is highly motivating.

For children, the activities are presented in a planned, formal sequential way, but teachers are encouraged to be flexible in their own creative approach to their delivery. Each circle meeting has five steps which take the group through an 'introductory phase', that relaxes the group and prepares them for the middle phase which is an 'open forum' when the 'work' of the session is discussed. The meeting then culminates in a 'closing phase' where the children engage in activities that lighten the mood and ensure that everyone feels safe and comfortable. The five steps are:

1   Meeting Up – Game

This can be a fun warm-up to help the children relax, release tension, and feel the joy of being together with each other. These starting rituals are vital to create the right supportive climate. For some classes it is best not to start with a highly energetic game; instead, a more relaxing activity such as a guided fantasy may be chosen.

2   Warming Up – Round

In order to encourage the children to listen to each other, a verbal activity is introduced. During a round, a conch or talking object is used to symbolise good listening. Whoever is holding the object has the right to speak uninterrupted. The talking object is then passed to the next person. Any child who does not wish to speak may say 'Pass' and hand it on.

3 Opening Up – Forum

This phase is an opportunity for discussion. Any subject that seems relevant to the needs of the class may be introduced and children contribute problems, opinions, and issues by raising their hands. If appropriate, action plans can be formulated or reviewed. During this time, it is possible to introduce drama and role-play in order to deepen children's understanding. This middle phase is vital for encouraging children to develop a belief in their ability to make responsible choices and decisions.

4 Cheering Up – Celebrating Success

It is important to help children to move away from the issues of concern raised in the middle phase. Children are encouraged to talk about their successes and strengths and to give praise to each other for any improvements or qualities they have noticed.

5 Calming Down – Closing Ritual

This is a winding-down phase that ensures that a proper feeling of closure is achieved.

One of the main principles of Quality Circle Time is that all children should be included and equally valued within the circle. It is, therefore, important that any child with special educational needs, or disability, is given the necessary support to enable them to participate in Circle Time. If this means one-to-one support, the adult involved should be fully briefed on the appropriate level of support for that child. For a child whose development is delayed, this might involve simplifying an activity in order to make it meaningful. It is no use simply including a child in the circle if that child is unlikely to gain anything from the activities; you need to find ways to help the child to participate as fully as possible.

The maintenance of high self-esteem requires not only that we experience positive feedback and success but also that we are protected from the damage of bad experiences. This is most effectively achieved in environments where everyone is clear about the behaviours that are expected and that have well-defined boundaries. The Quality Circle Time Model adopts an ecosystemic approach that encompasses all aspects of school life and thus provides the consistency of expectation, sanction and reward that gives staff and children a secure environment in which they can concentrate on academic accomplishment. This involves the teaching of moral values through a code of behaviour called Golden Rules. Golden Rules are the means by which the values of Circle Time are extended into every area of school life. They are a way of bringing concepts of morality and responsibility into the forefront of the community. They enable all participants to become more aware of their right to speak, and of their responsibility to listen.

A system of privileges and sanctions is structured to reinforce the rules and this ensures that the ethos of the school is underpinned by a clearly understood morality. Participation in the system helps children to learn that communities are prepared to put time and effort into upholding moral values.

Many children's behavioural problems stem from the fact that they do not know how to play with each other. Break times can be experiences of fear, loneliness and boredom. Good practice means creating possibilities for all kids to join in a range of different activities. It also means providing quiet places for them to go. The Quality Circle Time Model does not proscribe how children play, but it does encourage them to find activities that they enjoy and to find ways of relating to each other in caring and inclusive ways.

We live in a society that values competency and academic success. We have a Government that is deeply concerned with raising standards. Many children struggle to establish and maintain a sense of worth and belonging under the resultant pressures. Self-esteem is clearly implicated in the achievement process and variations in self-esteem are closely related to the ability of many children to benefit from their education. Our children urgently need a trusting and communicative environment if they are to learn their worth and become motivated as learners. The Quality Circle Time Model has all the structural requirements necessary to raise self-esteem and thereby promote motivation and the desire to strive for success.

Further reading

The following are useful books that explain the principles of Quality Circle Time more fully and give session plans that are designed for this age group:

Here We Go Round, Quality Circle Time for 3–5 year olds, Positive Press, ISBN 0-9530122-1-2.

Quality Circle Time in the Secondary School, David Fulton Publishers, ISBN 1-85346-616-6.

Ring of Confidence, A Quality Circle Time Programme to Support Personal Safety for the Foundation Stage, Positive Press, ISBN 0-9540585-1-8.

Stepping Stones to Success, A two year Quality Circle Time Programme for Early Years, Positive Press, ISBN 0-9540585-0-X.

References

Burns, R., 1982, *Self-Concept Development and Education*. Holt Reinhart & Winston, London.

California Task Force to Promote Self-Esteem and Personal and Social Responsibility, 1990, *Toward a State of Self-Esteem*. Sacramento, California State Department of Education.

Lawrence, D., 1996, *Enhancing Self-esteem in the Classroom* (2nd edn). PCP Ltd, London.

Owens, T., Stryker, S. and Goodman, N., 2001, *Extending Self-Esteem Research*. Cambridge University Press, Cambridge.

Wetherall, M. and Maybin, J., 1996, in R. Stevens (ed.) *Understanding the Self*. Sage, London.

Tract 19

Meeting the challenge of change

James Park, Director of Antidote, gives reasons for fostering emotional literacy in schools

Back in 1997, psychotherapist Susie Orbach called upon policy-makers to pay more attention to the promotion of emotional literacy in our schools. She declared:

> Educators are charged with making society for the next generation. The emotional aspects of the environment that children experience in school become deeply imprinted on them. They affect their relation not only to study but to work, to community, to the wider society. Post-school experiences may be approached with excitement, confidence or dread depending in part upon what has happened in the school environment.
>
> (Antidote 1997)

Seven years on, there are still some who mis-hear this call as indicating a disinterest in academic standards or advocacy of let-it-all-hang-out individualism. Others have taken up the idea of emotional literacy in only a limited way, as a tool for enabling particular groups of students to work through feelings of anger, shame or distress that get in the way of their learning. Increasing numbers, however, recognise that emotional literacy describes a vital part of any strategy for equipping young people with those learning-to-learn qualities described by Ruth Deakin-Crick (see Tract 32).

Points of disagreement

The disagreements arise from different understandings of the relationship between thinking and feeling. Sceptics about emotional literacy tend to view thinking as a 'higher' function, which may need to be cultivated at the expense of emotional understanding. Advocates of emotional literacy, by contrast, point to recent neurobiological research (Damasio 1996; LeDoux 1998) which suggests that thinking and feeling are inextricably intertwined; that you cannot remember anything significant, discriminate between conflicting arguments, have a creative idea or solve a significant problem without having access to the information that emotions provide.

Those who hold the latter position conclude that schools need to work out strategies for enabling young people to think about their emotions and use feelings to enrich their thinking. Only in this way will their students come to understand the human aspects of what they are studying – how the interactions between people are shaped by language, articulated in literature and have their influence on the movements of history and the patterns of scientific discovery. Emotional literacy enables young people to bring the whole of themselves to their learning, and in the process to develop the resourcefulness they need to negotiate their way through the challenges that will confront them, whether in their families, their workplaces or their communities.

Promoting emotional literacy

How, though, is emotional literacy to be promoted? The answer does not necessarily lie in training programmes for teachers or students. Emotional literacy is best conceived as a practice – something that people do together, rather than something that individuals have more or less of – and as a positive quality that needs to be continuously promoted across the whole school, rather than as the solution to a problem afflicting a particular group. Nor is there some emotional literacy norm that people need to be driven towards; the point of emotional literacy is to enable people with various ways of experiencing themselves and seeing the world to value each others' different experience of the world and to find a way of learning from and with each other.

While people clearly do vary in their levels of empathy and intuition, a large part of their capacity to show emotional understanding is dependent on the environment in which they find themselves. Do they feel safe enough to listen to themselves in a way that enables them to listen to others? Are there opportunities for them to articulate what they are experiencing in a way that others can hear and learn from? Do they feel that their experience can be valued for what it says about the situation in which the school community collectively find themselves? These are the critical factors in developing emotional maturity.

Emotional literacy is promoted when people are given opportunities to be themselves in the presence of others; to describe what they are experiencing without risk of censure or mockery, and with the prospect that what they reveal will have an impact on what then happens in and beyond the school. Every member of the school community has some capacity to determine whether a particular environment feels safe or risky. An emotional literacy strategy, therefore, needs to engage senior managers, teachers and other staff as well as students, helping them find ways to enlarge their own emotional understanding so that they in their turn can make it easier for others to build on theirs.

Individuals in the group

Emotional literacy enables individuals to strengthen their own learning capacity through the way they relate to others. They become more effective learners when they can allow what other people feel, think and know to inform their judgements, to stimulate their thinking, to challenge their conceptualisations. They are more likely to do so in an environment that continually draws people back to the important questions that face that learning community: What do we know? What will enable us to learn more? How can we contribute to the learning of each other?

The challenge for those wishing to promote emotional literacy is, therefore, to find ways of creating the sort of environment in which people can engage with each other. It is about *how* people do things more than it is about *what* they do. Students may attend weekly circle time sessions without ever feeling that they can raise there the issues that trouble them; they may acknowledge the availability of a peer support system but never think of using it to address their emotional difficulties, and never think of taking part in the opportunities offered by a school council to participate in shaping the school environment. Meanwhile, the teacher who encourages students to observe what is happening between them as they pursue significant questions in physics or chemistry, may open up great vistas of emotional understanding.

Somewhere to begin

The danger of emphasising the potential ubiquity of emotional literacy is that it ends up nowhere in particular. The challenge is to know where to begin. At Antidote we have developed a tool – the Emotional Literacy Audit (ELA) – which is designed to address this challenge. It has several purposes. One is to get a conversation going about how what is happening emotionally in a school affects people's ability to teach, to learn and generally to thrive. Another is to identify strategic places for each layer of the school – senior management, staff, students – to address in order to enhance the practice of emotional literacy. The audit also serves as an instrument for regularly monitoring shifts in the school's emotional literacy so as to help people sustain and build on any progress that is made (Antidote 2003).

Primary case study

The application of this approach in primary and secondary schools has demonstrated the value of an approach that seeks to build on *good practice* that is already going on in the school, to address every element in the school as part of a whole system, and to draw out the creativity of teachers and students in developing new practice.

At one primary school in an ethnically mixed area, we discovered that staff felt they were not communicating well with each other, and that students were feeling perplexed and bemused by the logic of the systems set up to control their behaviour. We responded to the staff issues by encouraging the development of a new team structure and changes to the ways in which meetings were run. For students, we helped set up a peer mediation programme through which students could explore more deeply their relationships with each other and look at how they could start taking responsibility for their own behaviour and learning.

As we explored the impact of these changes in the classroom, it became apparent that staff felt the regular circle time sessions they held in class were not having the desired effect on the depth of communication between young people. There were too many invisible children unable to find a voice in the circle, and too many topics that felt too sensitive to be spoken about. We responded by offering all staff some training in the use of enquiry and dialogue as a way of stimulating young people's interest in each other, and in what they were learning. Several teachers started using the approach regularly across the whole curriculum. Thanks partly to the prior work on staff communication, they found themselves able to support each other in finding new ways of using enquiry to transform the emotional climate of their classrooms.

Secondary case study

One of the most surprising discoveries from our work is how often teachers who evolve innovative ways of responding to the emotional needs of their students keep this work to themselves. Even when a headteacher has a declared sympathy for emotional literacy, teachers can feel that such practices are somehow 'against the rules', and fear that they will bring down the wrath of Ofsted inspectors if they are revealed.

At one secondary school where we were working, it was a full year after we had completed our survey of the school's emotional literacy that we were able to convene a group of such teachers to look at how they could share their practice with colleagues and work on ways of further enhancing it. After they had been talking together for a while, they started reflecting on how they could help each other address the difficulties they were having.

There was one class in this school where the boys seemed unable to listen to anyone and the girls had become largely passive. Our interest in discovering what it was about the situation for this class that was causing such behaviour led to us designing a group day for all students, their head of year, their tutor and two of their subject teachers. During the morning, the young people engaged in a team-building exercise, while their teachers awarded points when they saw evidence of students using teamwork skills. The afternoon was spent unpacking the links between what had happened in the exercise, and the real life of the class. This led to a rich discussion on the issue of gender difference and how suspicion develops across genders. As this conversation continued in classes over subsequent weeks, staff began to find that they had less difficulty being heard. Boys became more engaged in their learning, and the girls started to participate more actively.

Bedding down emotional literacy

Each of these projects provides a laboratory for the development of processes that can be disseminated across the school and more broadly. In the process, they are changed and adapted to reflect the different age profiles, personality mixes and emotional histories of the groups which take them up. For an emotional literacy strategy to work, the various strategies that evolve need to be continuously integrated into other parts so as to bring about a cumulative benefit. The work needs to grow through people seeing that it energises students to learn, and enables staff to enjoy working collaboratively and creatively together.

Ultimately, fostering emotional literacy in a school requires the maintenance of an ongoing conversation across the community through which people can articulate what is happening for them. When this conversation goes well, it enables new discoveries to emerge and relationships to deepen in a way that allows people to develop the courage and creativity they need to grapple with difficulties and to work through whatever gets in the way of their realising the richness of their thinking and feeling selves.

For more information about Antidote and emotional literacy, call 0207 247 3355, email emotional.literacy@antidote.org.uk *or look at the website* www.antidote.org.uk

References

Antidote, 1997, *Realising the Potential: Emotional Education for All.* Antidote.
Antidote, 2003, *The Emotional Literacy Handbook.* London, David Fulton Publishers.
Damasio, A. R., 1996, *Descartes' Error. Emotion, Reason and the Human Brain.* Papermac.
LeDoux, J., 1998, *The Emotional Brain: The Mysterious Underpinnings of Emotional Life.* London. Weidenfeld & Nicolson.

Tract 20

Curriculum, schooling and the purpose of learning

Tony Breslin, Chief Executive of the Citizenship Foundation, develops the concept of schooling in an age of lifelong learning

Mapping the challenge: contexts and opportunities

Any serious response to the question 'What are schools for ...' must begin by acknowledging the current position of the education system in the UK. This position is characterised by five key features:

- The need to respond to a complex and often contradictory policy agenda.
- A previously unheard of level of political scrutiny which increasingly is found across public services throughout Western Europe.
- A consequent concern with performance targets and sometimes pointless or counter-productive, measurement.
- An infrastructure, at secondary level, designed for the needs of the nineteenth rather than the twenty-first century.
- The end of deference that previously sustained such a schooling structure.

Furthermore, the traditional bureaucracy born of these pressures, has lost touch with what the bells, registers, forms, reports, inspections and tables are actually about: students' learning and their subsequent fulfilment as effective, successful citizens. In short, the stuff of the educational system has overwhelmed our proper concern with the purpose of learning. And *learning* is what schools should be about.

There are, though, grounds for optimism as practitioners, politicians and theorists of all persuasions and backgrounds begin to move beyond traditional models of schooling and assessment. At the heart of this new thinking lie four concerns:

- the nature of the curriculum and its content;
- the way individuals learn and what this means for the teaching process;
- the tools we need to assess these new kinds of curriculum and learning;
- the schools, colleges or learning institutions that we need to support the new approaches to curriculum, assessment and pedagogy.

Policy and practice: pressures and contradictions

I start with a tension at the heart of the current educational agenda: the stress between raising achievement and maintaining inclusion. The common-sense response advanced by policy-makers and politicians is that these two go hand in glove: raise achievement and inclusion takes care of itself. The reality is that this has never been the case. As any teacher in a 'challenging' school will testify, the more successful they are with the 60, 70, 80%, the more excluded the 40, 30, 20% become and, critically, in terms of the current focus on 'school improvement', the more marginal the gains. Schools that place student participation and citizenship at the core of their practice can begin to address this tension.[1] However, no single solution such as this can fully address so complex and enduring a problem.

There is, of course, a place for achievement-focused improvement strategies and targets when there is real under-performance in the system. However, when every teacher, especially those in the toughest schools (a more honest euphemism than 'challenging'), is working effectively to the limit of their abilities, the search for further gains in performance leads only to a crisis in professional morale.[2]

Moreover, when school improvement measures – league tables, Ofsted inspection reports, and performance management – are tied to 'parental choice', the situation is made worse. The strongest schools select their children from what Marx might have called 'a reserve army of middle class parents'. The outcome is not a vibrant market in schooling but a state of damaging competition where the strong gain at the expense of the weak.

Most schools do not provide a natural setting for learning. They are hierarchical, strongly departmentalised, and organised around the needs of the longest established academic disciplines (but little else). They lay down a school day, marked out by bells into a set of 'same size' lessons in which subjects as diverse as Art, Citizenship and Technology struggle to prosper. In short, the modern secondary school is closest in institutional form to the nineteenth-century prison or psychiatric hospital, industrial in structure and military in discipline.[3] The impact of such places is fourfold:

1 The organisational form moulds both the content and the form of the curriculum.
2 It limits the creativity of both the students and the teaching force, reinforcing subject demarcations within the latter group and pastoral demarcations within the former.

3   Critically, the overall institutional effect is to maximise the feeling of change while minimising its impact and effectiveness.
4   Finally, the excessive focus on structures and rules sits uneasily with the decline in deference that has marked the past 50 years.

This explains why teachers' unending struggle to effect change produces little more than a curriculum for an early twentieth-century grammar school. It also explains why youth workers leading lunch-time and out-of-school hours-programmes often succeed where those who are teacher-trained and school-conditioned fail.[4]

Grounds for optimism: the new curriculum agenda

Now at last the curriculum is on the agenda. It needs to be, for our curriculum is a statement of the values, skills and knowledge (the order is deliberate) through which we induct the next generation; the learning baton that we seek to pass on. As Bart McGettrick reminds us (Tract 8) the curriculum must be at one with the purpose of education if, as a society, we are to achieve our educational goals. Evidence of this new interest in curriculum is clear from the following:

- The launch of the National Literacy and Numeracy Strategies and their progression through to the secondary school have raised curricular and pedagogical debates of the highest standard, whatever the impact of the strategies themselves.
- The focus on concepts like 'Thinking Skills' in the Key Stage 3 Strategy and the broader emergence of Philosophy for Children[5] or 'P4C'.
- The emergence of a real debate about upper secondary learning and Further Education, notably through the 14–19 agenda. This discussion is at last showing signs of evolving from a discussion about *qualifications* to one about learning entitlement or *curriculum*.
- The beginnings of a discussion about the nature, purpose and timing of assessment and in particular (through the 14–19 initiative) some support for a gradual move from 'all at once' to 'just in time' assessment models.
- The persistence of interest in a whole range of new types of 'subject' that range from Citizenship, Enterprise Education and Financial Literacy through Key Skills to the broader range of vocational programmes and Work Related Learning schemes. Proponents of these approaches are beginning to form purposeful alliances that may ultimately see them demanding a significant re-engineering of the secondary school day.
- The growth of 'learning to learn' models championed by organisations like the Campaign for Learning[6] and the University of the First Age which focus as much on the how and where of learning and of curriculum as on the content 'delivered'.

- The growth of knowledge about access curricula (Campbell 2004) and alternative curricula. This might be through Family Learning programmes, ESOL models, SEN practice, work in Pupil Referral Units and programmes led by Connexions Services and in the Youth and Community sectors.
- The recent championing of 'subject specialism' by the current Secretary of State for Education, Charles Clarke.[7] The latter, of course, while commendably building on the network of teachers' professional bodies, is a double-edged sword: the challenge in the school of the future is to get teachers to 'talk' across rather than simply within subject boundaries. Nonetheless, a debate about 'subject' is a debate about curriculum and that is a significant move forward.

Association with the 'slow' or 'unsuccessful' learner taints much of the above. Work Related Learning and Vocational Education programmes, in particular, are often presented as deficit models not entitlement frameworks for all. This view overlooks, for example, the narrowness of the traditional GCSE dominated Key Stage 4 curriculum; not so much the breadth of 8–10 subjects as 8–10 variations on a theme. Nonetheless, these discussions are valuable because they go beyond curriculum itself in the demands that they make on curriculum frameworks and therefore on the structure of schooling itself. As such, they lay a foundation for moving secondary schooling forward.

From school improvement to school transformation: towards the future school

The current 'targets good'/'targets bad' debate, which is in danger of opening up a chasm between so-called educational radicals and those concerned with the realities of making policy, does none of us any good. Where ground is to be made up, targets have (and have had) their proper place, but we are in danger of becoming locked in the psychology of a targets culture. We need to move *beyond* targets and school improvement to models of school *transformation*. In plainer talk we need new types of school for a new era. What follows is a personal vision of the impact that a reformed curriculum would have on schools *of the future.* I would contend along with other contributors to this book that a 'Citizenship School'[8] is likely to be:

- based around a curriculum which places the knowledge, values and skills of citizenship explicitly at the heart of its curriculum (more democratic and less hierarchical);
- structured around a model of the school day that is as supportive of the extended activity in Citizenship, Art or Work Related Learning as it is of the traditional Mathematics or History lesson and, therefore, more inclusive and multi-faceted in its approach to learning, language and the curriculum;

- broader and less age related in its approach to assessment, balancing examination with accreditation and promoting formative over summative models, such that the focus shifts from the assessment *of* learning to assessment *for* learning[9];
- family friendly, community focused and child centred and, therefore, both rich in the range of ways that it engages *with* the community, parents and families and more accessible *to* them during standard school hours, at the weekend and in evenings;
- 'in tune', as a result, with the evolving needs of the communities that it serves but not insular in this support;
- multi-occupational and multi-professional in its staffing with more non-teachers supporting the curricular and pastoral life of the school (notably mentors, coaches, classroom assistants and counsellors);
- less of a total 'institution' with softer boundaries and more entry points for a wider range of participants; in short, less of a 'school' and more of a 'community learning centre';
- in a lifelong and *life-wide* learning age, a starting and staging point on an individual's learning career, not the sum total of it;
- as such, one of many learning facilities in a community, not the sole one.

This may seem like an incredible wish list. The truth, though, is that many schools are developing different aspects of the above and with great success. Here, the success of Deptford Green School in South London provides but one example of many schools that have used Citizenship as an engine of such change. Thomas Telford School in Shropshire provides a similar example where the vocational curriculum and ICT are the *curricular* drivers of this transformation.

Making change work: a modest proposal

If mere 'improvement' is challenging, 'transformation' (that is, real and substantive change) can be positively threatening. But teachers and school leaders have never rejected change, just those forms of change that drain energy and lead nowhere. The ingenuity and creativity of teachers should not be squandered; it must be translated into a resource for practitioner led and context informed curriculum development. It should be cast within the framework of a National Curriculum that, following the style of the current Citizenship requirement[10] sets out the core entitlement but does not define every detail of the content.

The energy of teachers needs to be harnessed to create the kind of schools we want in five, ten or 20 years time. Beginning now with a cluster of ten or 20 innovative and willingly linked schools from different settings might allow us to test the proposals set out above and elsewhere in this book. The RSA's recent *Opening Minds*[11] project with its focus on the efforts of six schools to develop a new competencies based curriculum provides a precedent for this kind of collaborative and experiential approach to innovation and we need to build on it.

Teachers don't resist change that works. They *seek* it. We might, at last, be close to a starting point.

Notes

1 Hannam, 2001.
2 Johnson and Hallgarten, 2002.
3 Breslin, 2002.
4 Dalton, Fawcett and West Burnham, 2001.
5 Ord, 2004, forthcoming.
6 Lucas and Greany, 2000.
7 DfES, 2003.
8 I have taken the title from *Citizenship School*, Alexander, 2001.
9 Campbell, 2004.
10 DfEE, 2000, QCA, 1998.
11 RSA, 2003.

Tract 21

Brave new e-world

John Potter, Editor, explores the implications of e-communications for the future of learning and the shape of schools to come

'The medium is the message.'

(Marshall McLuhan)

When schools hook their pupils to the net, they are opening the door on a new world where nothing will ever be quite the same again. The newly emerging e-technologies affect every aspect of life, including our values, politics, relationships and expectations for the future.

Jermaine's Day (Key Stage 3)

Jermaine arrives at school on the bus at about 08.30; his first task will be to register using his smart card. Although he has a tutor group room this is used for PSHE time and the class do not have to spend time registering as this is done automatically. Jermaine's first lesson today is English so he goes to Ms Wilson's classroom. The class are studying poetry. Ms Wilson starts the lesson using an interactive whiteboard with a presentation, 'word challenge'. By the end of the lesson Jermaine has his own version of the poem's text, saved in his English folder on the school server, complete with his thoughts on the poem alongside teacher's comments.

Source: Adapted from *Fulfilling the Potential*, DfES.

In Dudley – depicted in 1832 by the artist J. M. W. Turner as a town at the cutting edge of the industrial revolution – a second technological revolution is taking place. There are plans for 40,000 learners, adults as well as young people, to be networked through hand-held pcs (PDAs with new software) that will connect them to each other, their teachers/facilitators, their school databanks, the web and the world. Here, in microcosm, is the change that will transform everything. These children and adult learners will enjoy access to *choice* and personal learning that is both unprecedented and likely to shape the development of education for the coming fifty years. Here is a gateway to global learning and excellence in the *local* school that does not require parents and children to make damaging choices between competing institutions. (See Tract 23.)

Susan Greenfield, the neurologist, points out that 'IT will dominate the classroom in the future, not simply as a teaching aid, but as transforming the way we think.' She then asks, 'If computers are voice-interfaced, will there be any need to read or write? Moreover, if interaction with computers entails hypertexting and manipulation rather than reflection or abstract reasoning, will school children think in a different way? Furthermore, instant access to an infinite number of facts will mean that we should change our priorities away from learning in the traditional sense, and more into marshalling information and turning it into knowledge.'

Jermaine's Day: Break

First break and Jermaine goes to the admin area to top up the credit on his smart card. As well as being used for registration the smart card acts as a debit card for school lunches. He inserts money into the cash point and the credit to this value is added to his card. He will now be able to 'swipe' his card to pay for his lunch.

Source: Adapted from *Fulfilling the Potential*, DfES.

E-technology is transforming the way we work, relax and relate. It enables us not only to do some things faster or with less effort; it prompts us to do them differently, more flexibly and under quite new sets of conditions and expectations. E-living prompts us to relate to one another in new ways. Each day brings fresh possibilities for emailing, messaging, texting, beaming, chatting, shopping, voting, e-learning, file-sharing and, last but not least, on-line dating. Above all, we have increasing, almost instant, access to the largest data banks that have ever been assembled.

A different view of the world

This cornucopia of electronic possibility gives us a different view of the world. More of us work from home or collaborate on shared projects with colleagues from around the world. We retrieve, manipulate and disseminate information in ways that only a few years back were accessible only to major companies, universities and government departments. By the same token we encounter (or can perpetrate) new kinds of crime and nuisance, spamming, hacking, fraud, theft and pornography. Information and computer technology (ICT) has generated an interconnected galaxy of relationships that has changed forever the way in which networked people perceive and engage with the world.[1]

Jermaine's Day – Textiles

Design and Technology is next and Jermaine is working on a Textiles project designing and making a novelty notebook cover. Jermaine has researched his design ideas and made rough sketches of a logo by hand. He then produced his final version using a CAD package. He is now ready to embroider his designs using a computerised sewing machine. Using a video camera, linked to a projector trained on to a machine, his teacher demonstrated how to thread the sewing machine. The large screen display gave all the class a good view of what she was doing.

E-learning

Effective E-ducation grows from the whole matrix of electronic communications that are used to shape, manage and deliver learning across and beyond the curriculum. ICT makes possible new and more flexible learning environments. It opens up fresh connections between pupils and educators, parents, and the local and wider community. Schools are increasingly designing their intranets to develop the curriculum, provide individual learning plans and engage with the world beyond their gates.

Interactive whiteboards create fabulous opportunities for young pupils to experience together fresh ways of acquiring and responding to information. Video-streaming offers pupils the chance to attend live seminars with famous people and to interact with them. The extensive educational output of the major television companies and print media offer the best and most up-to-date information about what is going on in the world.

Jermaine's Day – Lunch

It is now time for lunch. Jermaine phones his Mum to check that they are still meeting each other at their local City Learning Centre (CLC). His Mother uses the Centre to brush up on her ICT skills following a recent Parents On-line presentation. She is a school governor and wants to be able to keep in touch with the other school governors, the headteacher and teachers via email and be able to log onto the governors section of the school's website.

Jermaine uses the Centre's modern foreign languages facilities. He is learning Italian which his school does not offer on the current curriculum.

E-ducation enables schools more effectively to co-ordinate their internal activities, refine timetables, create individual learning plans and give students and parents access to their own records and archives of their work. By the same token ICT enables schools to enter into partnerships with one another and form links (and related projects) between town and country, north and south, the UK and the rest of the world.

This enables two things to happen which support policies and initiatives recommended elsewhere in this book. First, it enables schools in a given locality to work closely together. ICT will facilitate Tim Brighouse's vision of collegiate schools (pp. 119) working together in a given town or borough. It also enables Tony Hinckley (pp. 148) to describe how e-technology will enable educators in his school of the future to:

- manage the common elements of their curriculum;
- create independent learning centres that are shared between several institutions and have access to shared e-resources;
- monitor the activities and learning of students who are free to move from one site to another.

Jermaine's Day

After lunch Jermaine returns to his lesson to complete his textiles project. He is really pleased with the final product but now he has to carry out a critical evaluation of how the project has gone. Using one of the PCs in the classroom he downloads a template his teacher has produced which provides help on how to evaluate what he has done.

Second, e-learning can foster a global approach to learning in all subject areas and across the school as a whole. Twinning, international partnerships and the sharing of people, ideas and resources is not simply desirable but necessary in an age where boundaries are becoming more permeable, ideas more accessible and the future of the planet more problematic (see Tract 7).

Fulfilling the potential

Research shows that e-learning raises standards across the board[2] and that ICT can have a direct positive relationship to pupil performance – equivalent in some subjects to half a GCSE grade. The evidence also indicates that primary schools with good ICT resources achieve better than schools with poor ICT resources, even when compared with schools of a similar type, and irrespective of socioeconomic circumstances or the quality of management.

In just over four years over 99% of schools have been connected to the Internet, of which over a quarter have a fast 'broadband' connection. The

---

Jermaine's Day

The last lesson of Jermaine's day is Science. He is currently studying a unit of work on heating and cooling. Jermaine's science teacher, Mr Watts, introduces the lesson on changing state by showing the class how to change water to ice, by evaporating ether from a beaker standing in a film of water.

Jermaine and his friend use a beaker, a data logger, temperature sensor and laptop to record what happens when the ice gradually melts and the water heated. They use a laptop and projector to display and share the results with the whole class. His homework on the topic is available on the school intranet.

National Grid for Learning has been developed into the world's largest portal of indexed educational content while customised portals are being created for key groups such as young people, teachers, parents and school governors. Curriculum Online has been launched, providing teachers with a showcase of high quality digital resources from public and private sector suppliers. Nonetheless, research in 2002 showed that there is still far to go in many schools before every pupil has regular access to using computers[3] and every teacher shows e-confidence (see box).

An e-confident school

An e-confident school will show evidence of:

1   High levels of staff confidence, competence and leadership.
2   Re-engineered teaching, learning and assessment, integrating effective use.
3   Leading and managing distributed and concurrent learning.
4   Effective application within organisational and management processes.
5   Coherent personal learning development, support and access – for all leaders, teaching and non-teaching staff.
6   Secure, informed professional judgement.
7   Appropriate resource allocation to ensure sustainable development.
8   Availability, access and technical support.
9   Pupils/students with high ICT capability.
10 School as the lead community learning and information hub.

As defined by the National College for School Leadership.

Building e-confidence

The Government is currently (2003–2004) promoting joined-up thinking and action between *teaching*,[4] *subject support* (through subject associations) and *learning* (ICT across the curriculum). The immediate challenges are: 1 opening up access to every pupil; 2 handling the sheer quantity of information; and 3 developing the confidence of teachers in using ICT.

Research shows that e-confidence is greatest in schools 'where leadership, resources and vision are key to the successful adoption of ICT'.

Challenges

The Internet galaxy comes with a health warning. Like every instrument for human achievement, ICT suffers from the drawbacks – sometimes dangerous drawbacks – of its advantages.

Behind the breathtaking development of electronic networks stand two fundamental questions: the first concerns social inclusion; and the second the purpose of education itself.

Access to the Internet is becoming essential for everything. The potential dark side of this freedom is, in Castell's words:

> The infrastructure of the networks can be owned, access to them can be controlled, and their uses can be biased, if not monopolised, by commercial, ideological, and political interests. As the Internet becomes the pervasive infrastructure of our lives, who owns and controls access to this infrastructure becomes an essential battle for freedom.

In this context e-learning and access to e-resources is and will long remain a political and human rights issue demanding eternal vigilance.

The second challenge prompted by e-learning takes us back to the question with which we began this book: What is the purpose of education? As ICT in schools develops, young people will gradually acquire the habits needed to master the e-world. They will learn how to learn, and to continue learning throughout life. They will achieve this through retrieving stored digital information, combining it in new ways and creating and applying fresh knowledge towards almost every conceivable end. The future school is in significant respects both defined and made possible by ICT.

This, however, is far from where we are now. Our vision of an e-confident future cannot be built on the outdated foundations of our Victorian school system. The symbiosis between e-learning and school reform must be taken seriously. Schools cannot become places of pupil-centred, life-long learning without the effective use of e-technology. By the same token e-learning is nothing without a pedagogy that nourishes each individual learner around her delight in developing her capacity to learn – on her own, with her peers and with the individual support of her teachers. The job of education reformers is to achieve *systemic change*. Without systemic change computers, intranets, websites and the electronic gizmos of tomorrow will be an expensive distraction. Where, however, systemic change is rooted in a clear and human educational purpose, ICT will prove to be the most powerful complement to the work of the educator that has yet been devised.

Notes

1 See Manuel Castells, *The Internet Galaxy: Reflections on the Internet, Business and Society,* Oxford 2001.
2 *Source*: Fulfilling the Potential: Transforming Teaching and Learning through ICT in schools. The research data and policy references refer only to England. DfES 2003, downloadable pdf go to www.dfes.gov.uk/ictinschools.
3 *Source*: MORI (Campaign for Learning, 2002 – CfL) research into the attitudes and practices of secondary school pupils with regard to Information and Communications Technology (ICT) – or 'e-learning' – at home and school. *Methodology*: 2,670 pupils in a nationally representative sample of 108 middle and secondary state schools in England and Wales were surveyed. The pupils were aged 11–16 and were in curriculum years 7 to 11. Interviewing was carried out through self-completion questionnaires with the whole class in one classroom period between January and March 2002.
4 DfES Enhancing Teaching and Learning.

Tract 22

Tests, exams, rumpus and brouhaha

John Potter, Editor, maps the issues behind the storms over testing and examinations, and points the way forward to a more ordered and effective approach

The rumpus over tests

My name is Seb, and I'm six years old. These are the things I like: X-Men 2, Man U and Game Boy Advance. These are the things I hate: fish fingers, playing the recorder and SATs.[1]

Seb enjoyed massive support over his attitude to SATs, the Standard Assessment Tests that were introduced under Margaret Thatcher to measure children's progress in maths, science and English that were required of pupils at the ages of 7, 11 and 14. (The science tests were later dropped for 7-year-olds.) The rumpus that eventually broke out between teachers and the Government over SATs had its roots in the disagreements that attended their origins. Professor Paul Black initially designed the tests as a formative assessment to help children learn and teachers teach. Margaret Thatcher, however, wanted something quite different: a simple summative test that would establish a pecking order between schools in the newly devised league tables. The prime purpose of SATs, therefore, shifted from assessment *for* learning to assessment *of* learning. Here lay the origins of the trouble to come.

Groundswell of hostility

By the autumn of 2002 the groundswell of hostility towards testing that had developed over the previous decade broke surface in an orchestrated rumpus led by the National Union of Teachers (NUT) and elements of the press. The strongest criticism was directed at imposing tests on 7-year-olds. The campaign was reinforced by research as well as by evidence of mounting unhappiness among children, their parents and teachers. A NUT Poll claimed that more than 90% of teachers wanted to boycott national tests for 7-year-olds and that 84% want to abandon all national testing at 7, 11 and 14 because of the narrowing focus the Government-led initiatives in literacy and numeracy have on the curriculum.[2]

Public opinion was divided. *The Mirror* headed a campaign against the tests and pointed out that parents feared for their children's health and well-being. The Association of Teachers and Lecturers (ATL) had earlier warned that SATs were in danger of driving pupils to take their own lives.[3] Senior academics from right and left cried 'Stop this testing lunacy'[4] and MPs on the Public Administration Select Committee criticised Whitehall for setting seemingly arbitrary goals for public services without evidence about what is realistic.

Research evidence

Most persuasive of all, however, was a sober report from a group of academics.[5] The Assessment Reform Group (ARG) had scrutinised the evidence from research into testing and came up with the significant conclusion that testing frequently does more harm than good. Testing of this sort, they argued, damages self-esteem and puts low achievers at a double disadvantage. Labelling children as failures affects how they feel about their ability to learn. It also 'lowers their already low self-esteem and reduces the chance of future effort and success'.

In other words the report underlined the obvious fact that tests of this sort help only those who succeed at them. The ARG proposed practical guidelines for positive action.

Teachers should:

- *involve pupils in decisions about tests;*
- *use assessment to convey a sense of progress in their learning to pupils;*
- *explain to pupils about the purpose of tests and other assessments of their learning;*
- *provide feedback that helps further learning in relation to teaching approaches.*

Policy makers and educators should:

- *adopt approaches that encourage self-regulated learning, including collaboration among pupils;*
- *cater for a range of learning styles cultivating intrinsic interest in the subject;*

- *put less emphasis on grades;*
- *promote learning goal orientation rather than performance orientation;*
- *develop pupils' self-assessment skills and their use of criteria relating to learning, rather than test performance;*
- *make learning goals explicit and helping pupils to direct effort in learning.*

Change in the air?

Charles Clarke responded positively to the outcry against SATs – and the threat of strike action by the NUT. He made it clear (May 2003) that tests, tables and targets will be retained, but he also stressed that he was listening to the anxieties of pupils, parents and teachers. He promised:

- a growing emphasis on value-added reports, not least in relation to children with special learning needs;
- teachers the opportunity to work with the local authority to set their own targets because 'setting targets in school can actually change children's lives';
- a new approach to assessing 7-year-olds 'where tests underpin teacher assessment rather than the two running alongside each other'.
- He asked for further reflection and proposals on ways in which the information in performance tables might be supplemented by information that gives a clear indication of the breadth and richness that are at the heart of good primary schools.

For the abolitionists this did not go far enough. For others, however, a breath of welcome change was in the air.

The brouhaha about exams

the exam system is jemmying schools further from the world they are supposed to be serving. It is trying to do too much. And it is a lousy preparation for life.[6]

> **Sticking plaster**
>
> 'What we've got now is a short-term sticking plaster. We need to plan alongside this for what we really want to do. We need a real overhaul, with more internal assessment, and people looking at that assessment to see if it's valid.'
>
> (Judith Norrington, director of curriculum and quality for the Association of Colleges)

The fuss about SATs leads to comparable questions about our present (2003) examination system. Ted Wragg, former professor of education at Exeter University, calls the current exam fever 'utter madness. The number of papers has gone up something like 10 times in the last dozen years. There used to be 2.4 million scripts a year, now it's 24 million.' He then adds that trying to improve the marking process is 'starting at the wrong end completely. There's no point in treating symptoms, you've got to treat the problem'.[7]

Our problem is that our elaborate structure of qualifications is like a house filled to the roof with furniture from generations of different owners with obsessive but contrary tastes. Our overloaded exam system is incoherent, inefficient and ineffective.

False distinction

'The distinction between academic and vocational ... is often made simply to mask what we believe might be shameful if said directly: that I personally would rather be a stock-broker than an able seaman, and that I would rather have my child playing first violin for the LSO than laying bricks.'

(Ken Boston, CEO of the QCA)

Incoherent and inefficient

The system is incoherent because it is a rag-bag of qualifications lacking a clear central theme and purpose. There is, first, the academic track (GCSEs – AS levels and A levels). Alongside this is the skills track leading from Entry level Certificates through to NVQ level 3. Somewhere in between are GNVQs that were designed to accommodate vocational studies. In addition there are various attempts to promote and recognise the key skills of communication, numeracy and computing.

Beneath all this confusion lies a serious – but too little discussed – tension between selection and inclusion. There are those who treat exams as the doorway to a select club. Others, however, regard an exam as a simple but important badge of competence which should be achieved as widely as possible. The attempt to put vocational qualifications alongside academic exams has done little to resolve this tension. In his address to the OCR Exam Board conference Ken Boston, England's qualifications chief, said that the distinction between academic and vocational is 'unhelpful and destructive'.[8]

Second, our exam system is inefficient. It is absurdly complex, needlessly bureaucratic and very expensive to run. Alongside the 24 million scripts submitted each year to independent examiners there are 3,700 specifications and certification covering almost 850 qualifications.[9] External examination does not come cheap and the current arrangements impose significant costs upon all involved.[10]

Ineffective

Third, and most serious of all, the system is ineffective. It does not achieve what it sets out to do. An assessment system typically has four objectives[11] as far as the individual learner is concerned. These are:

- diagnosis: helping young people to establish a baseline and understand their progress, strengths and development needs;
- recognition and motivation: recording and rewarding learners' progress and achievement;
- standard setting: defining levels and thresholds of achievement;
- differentiation and selection: enabling employers and HE to understand what young people have achieved, and how individuals compare to their peers.

Our present arrangements fail to deliver these objectives.

GCSEs in the firing-line

In many respects the General Certificate of Secondary Education (GCSE) has been a success story since its creation in 1986. It has provided a benchmark of achievement for 16-year-olds and a recognised qualification for those who leave school at that age. During the long hot summer of 2003 policy-makers congratulated themselves on a record number of exam entries (5.7 million). Furthermore the proportion of entries graded C or better rose slightly (from 57.9 to 58.1%).

Behind these encouraging results, however, lies a growing gap between those who do well and those who do badly.[12] More pupils than ever are gaining A grades, but the proportion who passed – gaining a G grade or better – fell. There is particular concern about falling standards in maths and the growing unpopularity of modern languages at GCSE and A level.

Furthermore, the percentage of ungraded pupils has risen (from 2.1 to 2.4%). In real terms these tiny percentages represent thousands of children who are likely to feel themselves let down by our qualifications system. Additionally, there is evidence that 10,000 14- and 15-year-olds go 'missing' from the school system every year. In 2002 more than 30,000 children left school with no GCSEs at all. These exams do not serve our less able children well.

Our system even fails to do well by our more able students. Tony Little, the head of Eton College, dislikes GCSEs because they get in the way of young people's preparation for higher level exams. He, therefore, proposed that his school should abandon them after 2007. Other people pointed out the danger of losing an intermediate qualification for the less academically able.

A bash at A levels

A levels have not escaped criticism. They are, according to the critics of your choice, too easy, or too narrow or simply failing to meet the economic and social challenges of our time. Purists claim that improved A level pass rates place the qualification 'in danger of becoming an exam candidates cannot fail'.[13]

Those who claim they are too easy – 'an exam you cannot fail' – point out that for 21 years A level results have been going up. They conclude that the exam is getting easier. In reality arguments about the relative difficulty of exams over the years is hard to establish as their content has changed. It is better simply to congratulate the students and their teachers and to ask the salient question: Do A levels enable universities (and employers) to distinguish the best from the rest?

A growing number of teachers and lecturers consider that they do not. Indeed some universities are thinking up their own selection tests. The Government's attempt to tackle this through the Advanced Extension Award has failed to lift off the ground. Geoff Lucas, secretary of the Headmasters and Headmistresses Conference, has offered five options to make A levels more selective (see box).

Extension papers: a higher tier at A level, available in all subjects.
Extension questions: instead of separate papers there could be more challenging questions as part of the A2 papers, open to all candidates.
Reporting achievement in terms of overall marks.
Recalibrating the A level scale: replacing present five grades with six grades
Norm-referencing the top grade: the new grade (A* or 1) could be awarded to the top 5% nationally achieving grade A in each subject.

These suggestions contribute to the debate but beg the question about selecting children according to their potential rather than their actual achievements. Many of the most successful A level candidates succeed because they have been well taught. Further evidence suggests that A levels have only a 60/40 chance of predicting academic success at university. There is a move[14] to introduce a weighting system in the results that will compensate for social and economic deprivation and focus instead on *potential*.

Too narrow

In most countries school leavers take exams that cover a broader range of subjects than is covered by the average two or three A levels. Proponents of breadth generally look towards a baccalaureate style examination, and their arguments are now taken seriously by the Government.

A Level Facts

- Only one pupil in 30 sat A levels when the exam was introduced in 1951.
- Since then the number of separate subject entries has risen from 103,000 to 750,537 (summer 2003).
- It costs the state £3,000 for a pupil to take three A levels.
- More than 100,000 pupils had grades reviewed in 2002 after a controversy over changing grade boundaries.
- After the review, fewer than 2,000 candidates got better results.
- In February 2003, Coventry university researchers found A level exams induce suicidal thoughts in 8% of students.

Source: TES 15 Aug 2003

Failing to meet the needs of the nation

A more recent criticism comes from those who notice the early signs of a flight from maths, science and languages towards the 'softer subjects' such as psychology, media studies. On the face of it, then, the A level system is failing to provide the nation with graduates who have the qualifications – in the sciences, maths and languages – that are most needed in a modern, world-class economy.

Back to basics

The Government invited Mike Tomlinson to lead an inquiry into what must be done about our exam system. He finally reported in the summer of 2004.[15] At the time of writing (January 2004) he has given an outline of his ambitious but careful programme of change. His initial proposals address almost all of the grounds for serious disquiet that have been set out in this and the preceding chapters. In his own words:

The Government's decision to consider reform of the 14 to 19 curriculum and qualifications represents a once-in-a-life-time opportunity to introduce change that puts the learner's interests first. In particular it provides an opportunity to:

- plan coherent curriculum pathways which provide for access and achievement by all students;
- have assessment which supports the curriculum and learning, rather than dictates or distorts them;
- have qualifications that provide a more complete picture of students' achievement, while providing differentiation for employers and higher education.

> The present fragmentation of qualifications ... inevitably results in many 14 to 19-year-olds following curricula which lack coherence and where one element of study has little or no relationship to the other. Further, the acquisition of an appropriate level of performance in key skills of communication, numeracy and computing is achieved by far too few young people.[16]

His central concern is to put the learner first. He and his working group envisage a coherent programme of related qualifications made up of:

- basic education, including the key skills of communication, numeracy and ICT;
- specialist learning, covering subjects or vocational/occupational courses;
- supplementary learning, which will support specialist learning and include higher order skills as needed and the extracurricular activities that develop the broader personal and employability skills.

These elements should fit within a single baccalaureate-style diploma. They would replace the existing exams, but a clear equivalence is outlined (see box) to help people understand the new system.

Diploma (BAC style)	Current equivalents
Level 3 Advanced Diploma	AS, A level. NVQ level 3. Advanced Extension Awards
Level 2 Intermediate Diploma	GCSE A*–C, Intermediate GNVQ, Level 2 NVQ
Level 1 Foundation Diploma	GCSE D–G, Foundation GNVQ, Level 1 NVQ
Entry Level Diploma	Entry level Certificates

This timely thinking proposes an exam system that is coherent, learner centred, well-balanced and administered locally. It offers a flexible ladder of qualifications that includes more than academic tests and can be challenging to the most able as well as supportive to everyone else. Qualifications will be portable and contribute significantly to lifelong learning. Tomlinson's approach provides a platform for wider educational reform and deserves the active support of educators, young people, parents and the wider public.

AGENDA FOR CHANGE

The real voyage of discovery consists not in seeking new landscapes but in having new eyes.

(Marcel Proust)

School governors are the 'grassroots government of education', responsible for policy and practice of their school. Governors need to know about key research findings on school improvement, motivation, self-esteem, emotional literacy and learning to learn.

For children to learn, schools need to:

- actively promote 'learning to learn' as an approach and set of skills;
- develop the five Rs of lifelong learning: Readiness, Resourcefulness, Resilience, Remembering, Reflectiveness;
- develop teacher's skills as learning facilitators;
- enable parents to participate in learning to learn courses and activities;
- create a learning environment using display, music and new technologies;
- provide pupils with drinking water, exercise and meditation;
- give pupils opportunities to debate, take responsibility, question authority and develop the habit of freedom;
- enable pupils to develop creativity and a moral sensitivity of caring;
- develop a whole-school approach to self-esteem including circle time, one-to-one listening, games and celebrations;
- foster emotional literacy and security for children and adults, through opportunities for reflection, speaking and listening in which personal experience and identity is valued;
- use the Emotional Literacy Audit to talk about emotional literacy, identify strategies for enhancing it and monitoring development;
- be inclusive and value everyone and their differences;
- create a curriculum as a statement of values, skills and knowledge (in that order) as a guide for schools rather than as a prescription;
- have curriculum framework that helps young people develop the skills and competencies they will need to make sense of life's complex uncertainties, using content (subjects) as the context;
- include thinking skills, enterprise education, financial literacy, key skills and broader work-related learning for all;
- put citizenship explicitly at the heart of the curriculum;
- encourage teachers to 'talk' across subject boundaries;
- free the timetable to support extended activity in citizenship, art or work-related learning to develop a more inclusive and multi-faceted approach;

- develop assessment *for* learning that:
  - *provides effective feedback;*
  - *actively involves pupils in assessing their own progress;*
  - *is used by teachers to improve learning;*
  - *records and celebrates achievement, thus increasing self-esteem and motivation;*
  - *helps students understand themselves as learners and develop autonomy;*

- make the school more accessible to parents, families and the community during standard school hours, at the weekend and in the evening;
- employ more non-teachers to support the curricular and pastoral life, notably mentors, coaches, classroom assistants and counsellors;
- use the Internet and worldwide web to support learning within and beyond school;
- move *beyond* targets and school improvement to models of school *transformation.*

Notes

1 Quoted from 'These tests make my head hurt', Jo Revill, *The Observer*, Sunday, 18 May 2003.
2 *Guardian*, Wednesday, 16 October 2002.
3 See Nathan Yates, *Mirror*, 20 May 2003.
4 James Tooley and Tony Edwards presented a joint platform in the TES on 6 June 2003.
5 Testing, Motivation and Learning from the Assessment Reform Group, University of Cambridge Faculty of Education, 2002. The work was carried out principally by Wynne Harden and Ruth Deakin-Crick.
6 Geraldine Bedell, *The Observer*, 18 August 2002.
7 'Too many exams fail the test', *Independent*, 5 May 2003.
8 Ken Boston, Chief Executive QCA, reported BBC 26 September 2003.
9 *Source*: Principles for Reform of 14–19 Learning Programmes and Qualifications, Chair: Mike Tomlinson (DfES July 2003). www.14-19reform.gov.uk.
10 Ibid., para 36.
11 Ibid., para 31.
12 Warwick Mansell, *Are we neglecting the least able?* TES, 22 August 2003.
13 Quoted by Conor Ryan in *Spinwatch*, TES, 15 August 2003.
14 'University grades deal to help poor', by Gaby Hinsliff and Kamal Ahmed, *The Observer*, Sunday, 21 September 2003.
15 For details of the proposed outline see www.14-19reform.gov.uk.
16 Mike Tomlinson, 'Putting the Learner First', TES Platform, 18 July 2003.

Chapter 4

Schools of the future

Letter to a local councillor

Dear Councillor,

Important choices

Local democracy has had a tough time over the past few decades. Central government has taken away many powers over education, giving some to schools, others to national agencies and keeping many for itself. At the time of writing (January 2004) there are suggestions that Whitehall should take direct responsibility for all state schools.

Local government has always had a pioneering role in education. That pioneering role is now more important than ever, at the level of the LEA, school and classroom. It is highly likely that over the next decade the role of local government will change as will that of schools; but the need for local democratic accountability has never been greater. The LEA today has a vital role in promoting debate and development about how schools can best serve the learning needs of children and their communities.

The national agenda for schools is likely to remain unsettled, as there is no clear framework or consensus about how the schools system should be run. Among the many different models competing for political support there is:

- **market choice,** advocated by James Tooley, Chris Woodhead and possibly the Conservative Party, that schools should be freed from state control and governed wholly by parental choice;
- the **comprehensive ideal,** advocated by CASE, Roy Hattersly and many in the Labour Party, that children of all backgrounds should go to the same local school, which should be the best it could possibly be, with no selection or private alternative;
- a **pluralist hybrid,** like that proposed by Tim Brighouse, or Tom Bentley's 'school without walls', in which the institution of a single school becomes less important than the commitment to offering children and parents choice and support within an inclusive framework.

We live in a time of flux over the framework for schools, in which we all need to rethink our assumptions in relation to what kind of institutions we need to support learning.

The Government has set out its strategy for secondary schools[1] around four key areas: specialist schools, leadership, the school workforce and partnerships beyond the classroom (Toby Greany and Cath Jones p. 12).

We tackle leadership and the school workforce in the next section. In what immediately follows we address the tension between liberty (choice) and equality (fairness) and the need in education – as in much else – to protect poor families from being excluded from the best in education.

Professor Tim Brighouse (Tract 24) offers an exciting model of co-operation between schools that deliberately address the need to match choice with fairness. Phil Street highlights the importance of Extended Schools which bring local community services into the heart of education. Roz Bird and Erik Stein demonstrate what is already being achieved in some pioneering rural and urban schools. Finally, Tony Hinckley, who has worked for a number of years on developing ideas and proposals for future schools, describes how a future school might incorporate the central proposals of this book.

Local communities, large and small, need and deserve schools that will enrich people's lives and reclaim democracy from an increasingly commercial and unaccountable education market.

John Potter and Titus Alexander

Note

1   Transforming Secondary Education, DfES, April 2003.

Tract 23

Winners and losers

John Potter, Editor and erstwhile Director of CSV Education for Citizenship, examines the tensions between equality, liberty and fraternity in our attempt to create an education system that is fair, accessible and sensitive to a wide range of needs and interests

> Education is the single most important factor in creating and sustaining a socially inclusive society.
>
> (David Blunkett, Secretary of State
> for Education and Employment, 2000)

Social inclusion is central to present (2004) policy. Centre-left Governments in Britain have systematically sought to redress the disadvantage of those who have neither the cash nor the cachet to win educational favours for their children. The 1944 Education Act – for all its academic elitism – was a massive achievement in opening up free state education to all. Later, the introduction of comprehensive schools recognised the dangers of segregating children into separate educational and social categories at the age of 11.

The Blair government, however, increasingly stresses the importance of choice. It has – to the discomfort of many of its own back-benchers – set out plans for 200 new City Academies. These are designed to enlarge parental choice, to give schools power of selection and free them from the direct control (interference?) of local authorities. The ensuing debate between equity and choice is likely to reverberate in our homes, staffrooms and public houses over the next few years.

When New Labour first came to power, David Blunkett, the then Secretary of State, gave four reasons why New Labour had set education at the top of its agenda.[1]

His first reason was economic: A modern, world-class economy requires a highly educated people. His final reason was moral and sprang from the need to make wise and informed moral judgements in a world facing new and complex issues. He instanced the environment, population growth and the advances in genetic sciences. His second and third reasons, however, concerned the twin goals of liberty and equality. 'Education is the single most important factor in creating and sustaining a socially inclusive society' he said and went on to add that 'education is [also] the great liberator. It can unlock what William Blake called those "mind-forg'd manacles". Education gives people greater control over their own lives.' In saying this, Blunkett harnessed freedom to fairness and placed choice on his egalitarian agenda.

In the marketplace Liberty and Equality pull in opposite directions. Your freedom to receive long-term hospital care is taken from my freedom to frequent Quaglino's or spend January in Acapulco. There is usually room for an element of compromise. The better off are prepared to pay some tax as the price for living in an ordered society with drains that work and police who catch criminals. But the underlying tension remains. The French revolutionaries invoked fraternity in their pursuit of liberty and equality. However, it takes a lot of brotherly love to make friends of fairness and freedom. It is here that the Government's education policy is running into trouble. Attempts to promote freedom of choice are at odds with efforts to create equal access to those choices.

The issue is fundamental to the way in which schools of the future will develop. It is also fundamental to the ways in which our public services generally are perceived and provided. Under the welfare consensus created by the first Labour Government public services were about citizenship and entitlement. The Government's self-appointed task was to banish the Giants of Want, Disease, Ignorance, Squalor and Idleness from the face of the nation. Public services would give every citizen, rich or poor, equal access to their entitlement. In a land of equal opportunity Giants would disappear. Freedom was welcomed as an escape from poverty and social injustice.

From civic entitlement to personal freedom

As people grew richer, politicians replaced Freedom *from* Want with Freedom *to* Choose. Margaret Thatcher transformed civil society into the social market. Successive Tory governments set about applying market principles to the provision of education services and the commercialisation of schools.

After 1997 – despite some changes – New Labour held firm to the market principle and sought further to develop it. Behind this attachment to the benefits of commerce lie two convictions. The first is that local government lacks the flexibility and efficiency of private enterprise, and so education along with prisons, transport networks and parts of the health service are best given to business to run. The second conviction is that parental choice between schools is the most effective way of ensuring that our children enjoy the education most suited to their different needs. From this mind-set surfaces an occasional contempt for 'bog-standard comprehensive schools.'

Public versus private provision

The case for markets in education needs unpicking. No single system of education provision is perfect. Public services have no monopoly of good practice or moral virtue. Nonetheless, the difference between public and private provision is important. Democratic government must account for its actions to the electorate on a regular basis. Business, on the other hand, is responsible only to its shareholders and indirectly its customers. Governments control civic space; businesses colonise commercial space.[2] Government is rewarded by public approval or rejection; business by private profit or loss.

Government policy under both the Tories and New Labour has been to move education away from the civic realm towards the private arena of the market.

Previous public education services are now in private hands and pockets. The democratic role of LEAs to provide, manage and review education services has been whittled away. At the time of writing private firms, largely staffed by ex-LEA employees, undertake 75% of school inspections. The fact that most of those now employed privately have worked previously for LEAs underlines the degree and nature of the change.

Professor Colin Crouch points out[3] that LEAs have been 'put in a position of competitors with rather than watch-dogs over contractors. This, combined with the long term nature of contracts, makes difficult any effective control of agent by principal'. He adds that 'The normal mode of delivering local education services becomes that of the privileged insider commercial firm; the firm becomes the only acceptable form of organisation; and public service becomes an anomaly within its own heartland.'

Tory and New Labour governments have schools to compete in an effort to drive up standards. In the shopping mall competition is driven by the price mechanism, which indicates value and rations the supply of goods and service. In the 'education market' the price mechanism fails because education is compulsory and most people are not prepared to pay the full cost directly. In consequence politicians have devised alternative price-tags. Policy-makers then take the analogy a step further by noting with dismay that their 'education outlets' are all selling the same goods. Their solution is to encourage schools to differentiate between their goods and services by offering specialist products such as engineering or the arts. Such reasoning lies behind the introduction of specialist schools and the recently announced city academies.

Specialist schools and academies

'We will create a new specialist system where every school has its own specialist ethos and works with others to spread best practice and raise standards', explained Education Secretary, Charles Clarke, when introducing the Government's commitment to transforming secondary education. His intention is that by 2006 there will be at least 2,000 specialist schools across the country.

City academies

'One glance at the faces of pupils attending the Capital City Academy in Brent, west London – formerly the failing Willesden High School – says it all. They reveal a sense of awe at what is being provided in place of the former shabby, ramshackle school.'

Independent, 2 October 2003.

Any maintained secondary school in England can apply to be designated as a specialist school in one of ten specialist areas: arts, business and enterprise, engineering, humanities, language, mathematics and computing, music, science, sports and technology. Schools can also combine any two specialisms.

By September 2003 nearly half of secondary pupils were being taught in specialist schools. David Miliband, the Minister for School Standards, told the Secondary Heads Association: 'We are replacing the old one-size-fits-all system ... specialist schools are a part of a mass movement to raise standards.'[4]

Specialist schools receive a capital grant of £100,000 along with additional income for each pupil. For some, however, there is a catch. Schools must raise £50,000 in sponsorship before seeking specialist status. This weighs against schools in rural and deprived areas.

City academies are another new type of school and they are central to Tony Blair's policy for 'Excellence and a choice for all in every community'.[5] Two hundred such academies are planned to be built or in the pipeline by 2010.

They are defined by the Government as 'all ability schools established by sponsors from business, faith or voluntary groups working in highly innovative partnerships with central Government and local education partners. Sponsors and the DfES provide the capital costs while running costs are met in full by the Government. The Academies programme aims to reverse the culture of educational under-attainment and to deliver real improvements in standards. All academies are located in areas of disadvantage. They either replace one or more existing schools facing challenging circumstances or are established where there is a need for additional school places. The Department expects LEAs to consider the scope for the establishment of Academies as part of their strategic plans to increase diversity in secondary provision and improve educational opportunities.

As with specialist schools, academies receive significant additional government funds along with significant funds from the sponsor. Academies are, in effect, state funded independent schools. They are set up as companies limited by guarantee with charitable status. Each academy is under the control of its governing body, which is responsible for its success. Academies are not accountable to the LEA, although an LEA appointee will sit on each governing body.

'... Paved with good intentions'

The Government aims to provide varied and appropriate opportunities for 'the many and not the few'. City academies sited thoughtfully in deprived urban areas aim to offer new opportunities for deprived children to learn in dynamic settings.

There is, however, a downside to virtual markets in education: they distort learning, exacerbate failure among struggling schools and erode the foundations of local democracy.

Distorting learning

SATs – originally intended to stimulate learning – are now used chiefly as the external indicators of a school's success. They provide 'price tags' for parents. This approach to testing discourages pupil achievement and provides parents with a potentially misleading picture of the quality of the school.

Struggling schools

The tension between freedom (choice) and equality (excellence for all) becomes a zero sum game where winners do well at the expense of losers. Government efforts to widen choice and reward success become the policies of the marketplace, where the fittest survive and the weakest are sent to the wall. This may be the best way to run a shopping centre. Education, however, is not a marketplace and 'constructive competition' robs Peter to pay Paul. Children in failing schools by definition have little opportunity to take their custom elsewhere. It is no accident that over recent years the gap between the most successful and least successful pupils has grown wider.[6] Since Labour came to power the chances of a bright child from a poor family becoming a high-flyer have worsened.[7]

Meanwhile, there is growing evidence[8] that around one in five ambitious state secondary schools use selective criteria deliberately to recruit children from successful middle-class families. Perhaps most significant of all, Ofsted, the Government's own quality watchdog, has warned against the distorting effects of the market.[9] It challenged Government support for the expansion of successful schools[10] and pointed to the risk of sending already struggling schools even more swiftly into a 'spiral of decline'. Ofsted at least is clear that the expansion of popular schools is by itself no solution to the problem of school improvement.

Democratic deficit

The Government has long proclaimed its concern about the erosion of democracy and the ebbing interest of the electorate, especially the young electorate, in politics. The extension of market principles to the places where citizenship once prevailed will damage democracy yet further. Local people, including local Councillors, face a massive task in challenging the corrosive effects of market values on once democratic institutions.

What can be done?

Colleges of schools

In Tract 24, Prof. Tim Brighouse describes how local urban schools can be grouped into a 'College' of institutions that *between them* provide the best that can be offered to children. In such a college there will be genuine variety and flexibility in physical and intellectual provision, but because every member institution shares responsibility for the success of the whole there will be less opportunity for the 'spiral of decline' to blight the prospects of the least able.

Extended schools and village colleges

These strengthen the bonds between schools and their communities and give practical point to the saying 'it takes a whole village to raise a child'. Such schools also offer a civic rather than commercial context in which learning can be inspired, managed and reviewed by local communities. In this context local government has an opportunity to rediscover its democratic role as the arbiter (if not always the provider) of the services its citizens choose to enjoy.

'Building schools for the future'

This is an ambitious Government commitment[11] to invest in quality school buildings that promote community learning, the strategic use of ICT and a more flexible curriculum. In February 2004 the first wave of 10 local authorities was announced, where the Government plans to invest £5.1 billion in school buildings in 2005–6.

The stakes are high. The Government plans 'to create environments that inspire and support both teachers and pupils, that drive innovation, and that deliver personalised learning: high expectations of every child, given practical form by high-quality teaching based on a sound knowledge and understanding of every child's needs'.

It is clear from conversations with heads that in some places at least this building programme will stimulate a collegiate approach between schools along with a radical policy for extending learning partnerships with local government, business and the community sector. There is already talk in some places of a constant shuttle of minibuses taking learners from one site to another to match educational needs with specialist resources.

With the right vision and commitment – especially from Heads, Governors and Local Councillors – this initiative could make a significant difference to the future of our schools.

Notes

1   *Raising Aspirations in the 21st Century*, a speech by the Rt Hon. David Blunkett MP, Secretary of State for Education and Employment at the North of England Education Conference in Wigan on 6 January 2000 (published DfEE London).
2   *Commercialisation or Citizenship: Education Policy and the Future of Public Services*, by Colin Crouch (Fabian Ideas 606, Fabian Society, March 2003). This monograph underpins and further explains the key points in this section.
3   Ibid., p. 55.
4   *Half of pupils in specialist schools*, by Richard Garner (*Independent*, 2 July 2003).
5   Announced 8 July 2004
6   *From rags to rags (and riches to riches)*, by Wendy Piatt, *New Statesman*, 18 August 2003, p. 21.
7   Ibid.
8   *MPs told of school admissions 'crisis'*, *The Guardian*, 11 September 2003.
9   Lucy Ward, education correspondent, reports on the conclusions of a Study of school place planning by the Office for Standards in Education (Ofsted), *The Guardian*, 14 October 2003.
10   On 4 August 2003 David Miliband announced that additional funding would be available from 2004–5 to support the expansion of successful and popular secondary schools.
11   For further details go to: http://www.teachernet.gov.uk/management/resourcesfinance andbuilding/funding/bsf/

Tract 24

The collegiate model: a family of city schools

Prof. Tim Brighouse, Education Commissioner for London, sets out a new model for comprehensive education

We must all work to make this world worthy of its children. They are 100% of its future. My wish for every child is that we would want them to be people with a strong sense of themselves and their own humanity, with an awareness of their thoughts and feelings, with a capacity to feel and express love and joy and to recognise tragedy and feel deep grief. We would want them to be people who, with a strong and realistic sense of their own worth, are able to relate with others, to co-operate effectively towards common ends and to view humankind as one, while respecting diversity and difference. We will want them to be people, who, even while very young, somehow sense that they have the capacity for lifelong spiritual and intellectual growth. Above all, we would want every child to cherish the vision of the person they are capable of becoming and to cherish the same potentiality in others.

I am also certain of two things. First, that our present urban system cannot provide this kind of education. Second, that in an urban area, however hard individual schools acting alone try to do so, collectively they will fall short of what is needed. Schools operating in isolation and in competition one with another necessarily cause changes in each other's compositions. Some schools will go down as others rise as long as we have parental preference, bus routes, and schools that have a practical limit on their size. So we need another answer to work towards in the large urban settings.

We need a more ambitious and comprehensive model for secondary education in our towns and cities. The word 'comprehensive' has begun to get in the way of productive debate. The media, sometimes assisted by those who should know better, have ensured that the term comprehensive has increasingly implied something vaguely second-rate. I therefore use the term 'collegiate' rather than 'comprehensive' to describe the new model for urban schools.

The comprehensive ideal was to give equal value to all sorts of human potential and activity within certain moral limits and principles. Comprehensive schools were never 'one size fits all', or 'bog-standard'. But it is only in the counties and market towns that we have a remotely comprehensive pattern of secondary schools. It has proved a well-supported and successful way to organise the schools. Nobody in Suffolk or Norfolk, in Oxfordshire or Cambridgeshire would want to turn back the clock. Children from all backgrounds and both sexes attend the local school. But only a third of secondary children attend schools in counties and market towns. The other two-thirds are in large towns, small cities and very large conurbations. In the latter actual comprehensive schools are few and far between.

We need to design a secondary schooling system which provides success for everyone and helps young equip themselves with the skill, dispositions and values to survive and thrive in a much more shifting, complex and diverse society.

We live in a high-risk world, but the secondary school is a low risk environment. We live in an age where nations have few national enemies, but are suffering an identity crisis and where ordinary citizens wonder about the interface of nationality and religion. In short, it is an age of uncertainty, with the traditional isolated secondary school struggling to remain place of certainty, but dealing with a client group of adolescents who can see that they are living in a world which is altogether different and to which their school seems not sure how to relate.[1]

My ideal is that all young people, whatever their 'home-base' school, whether in the state or private sector, take substantial periods of their education together. This would be within a collegiate framework which acknowledges that secondary education involves belonging to at least two institutions – the school and the collegiate to which it is attached.

In urban areas this has become essential in order to:

- overcome the huge and unfair divergence of experiences for pupils near the top or the bottom of the pecking order;
- match the diversity of schooling to the diverse needs of individual children;
- give all pupils equal access to the separate specialisms and expertise in specialist schools;
- give pupils from all schools the best possible access to high quality staff in shortage subjects;
- ensure that gifted pupils and youngsters with barriers to their learning come together and gain from the scarce expertise specialist staff;
- increase the curiosity and knowledge which comes from staff from different schools sharing opportunities for continuous professional development;

- take advantage of the progress in the learning technologies;
- increase the chances for any pupil in their individualised 14–19 learning pathway;
- mix and bring together, at least for a time, pupils of both genders from different social, ethnic and religious backgrounds to learn, to engage in sport, the arts, citizenship and debate about their future as international as well as national citizens.

If schools are left stranded in a 'devil take the hindmost' competition of 'beggar their neighbour', we shall not win the race between 'education and catastrophe'[2] for many of our disadvantaged youngsters. We must now encourage all schools in our great cities to move on from a culture of total independence to one which recognises the added value of carefully developed interdependence. This is what I mean by a 'collegiate' system.

A truly comprehensive secondary education in our conurbations would be one where all the youngsters, boys and girls alike, from the different faiths and ethnic groups are educated together for significant periods of their post-primary education. They will know that they are specially and equally valued, whatever their different intelligences or talents and backgrounds. They will know this because the school and other educational provision – the collegiate – they attend, will celebrate difference, whether of gender, race, or religion, but at the same time equally value different intelligences and talents.

What does collegiate mean in practice? A group of six or seven schools, including at least one comprehensive plus or selective school, a faith school and a special school, together with a major FE/HE provider. For some purposes and in some places perhaps an independent school as well.

These schools would be either loosely or tightly coupled. It would start with agreements about ensuring heads of department are off timetable at the same time across the collegiate so that ideas can be shared and curriculum and professional development organised: it could end with jointly published results and agreement to admit pupils post-Year 7 to the collegiate. As the model becomes more tightly coupled, the advantages increase for the pupils and for the realisation of the new comprehensive ideal.

Youngsters from all backgrounds would have the experience of learning together, whether in the classroom, the workshop, the music suite, the debating chamber, the workplace, the theatre, the laboratory, or in sport and athletics. They also will learn and meet each other 'virtually' using the full range of the new learning technologies which will help bind the collegiate together and enlarge its capacity. Such collegiates and their constituent schools may have 'associate members' – those who come from other collegiates for short or long courses that are offered there, or from those educated 'otherwise' by individuals or groups of parents.

How shall we move from here to there?

We need to harness the non-negotiable agenda of 'city academies', 'beacons', 'extended', 'training', 'advanced' and 'specialist schools' as the building blocks for the future. We need to find a way of tempting headteachers and their governors to join in. (For make no mistake about it, the pleasures and powers of independence and autonomy are considerable, especially when in living memory they were preceded by the shackles of dependence.)

Each school needs incentives to take part in the collegiate. What if the beacon status reflected 'leading edge practice' in a department or phase in different schools within a collegiate? What if each collegiate had its own residential centre? Or if incomers after Year 7 dealt with the admissions office of the collegiate and placed in any one of the constituent schools? Parents should be confident that the collegiate programme was so extensive that wherever their youngster was placed, she or he would have full access to the best that six or seven schools could offer between them.

The collegiate could have an international dimension, linked with schools in the other continents of the world.[3] The collegiate will include in its 'school plus' rationale a commitment to promote minority subjects and interests, cherish inter-faith and inter-cultural respect, promote European and global international citizenship, as well as that of the locality and the UK. The collegiate will be able to be inclusive where an individual school on its own cannot be. The collegiate will help overcome professional isolation so that there is a depth and richness of intellectual curiosity among the staff which will ensure that they are at the leading edge of practice in every discipline. Advances in the learning management and communication technologies (ICT) coupled with the non-metronomic timetable involving 'days' or 'weeks' of study, mean that a new and extra form of organisation is possible. In short, a collegiate can do what an individual school cannot.

We have all been frustrated by the debilitating side effects of league tables and competing institutions. The collegiate is a way of providing a solution by adding a dimension to a set of as yet unresolved urban issues and totally changing not merely its appearance, but also the ways by which the people in it will be able to work and realise their ideals. Inclusion could be a reality rather than simply an aspiration. The collegiate is the way of accommodating selection, diversity and equality of opportunity. As with all extra dimensions, it changes the appearance and the reality of a hitherto apparently intractable problem. Each collegiate will include the rainbow spectrum of different types of school which the Secretary of State has described. It is not the job of those who want to see urban schools succeed to protest, wring our hands, or tilt at windmills in the style of a latter-day Don Quixote. We need to provide opportunities for schools to see the advantage of richer interdependence that lies between the Scylla of dependence and the Charybdis of independence. We need to talk to some of the prestigious independent schools about how they might be prepared to associate with a collegiate. It is our job to ensure that any collegiate contains a representative group of comprehensive 'plus', selective, or super selective schools, as well as other secondary schools. We must lobby for conditions to be applied to all future city academies, specialist and advanced schools to be part of a collegiate, and that some of their extra community money is allocated to that end. It is our responsibility to see that all collegiates are involved with higher education institutions in initial teacher education and advanced study and that each 'collegiate' has at least two or three 'beacon' departments so they can take pride of being at the 'leading edge of practice and performance' which rubs off on their pupils[4] as well as their teachers.

If and when collegiates take hold, youngsters in such a collegiate will have a richer experience than many now do in their individual schools. We shall have come a little closer to realising the ideal of success for all our pupils in a truly inclusive environment where they have learnt the habit of lifelong learning and know they are all special and valued equally.

Ten challenges for creating schools of the future

This tract has sketched only a part of the picture – the first brush strokes. To complete the picture we shall have to look at ten inter-related facets of secondary education. The first four are learning, teaching,[5] curriculum and assessment,[6] of which the last powerfully influences the other three; and the fifth concerns the supply and quality of staff, especially teachers; a sixth is the internal organisational arrangements of the school, particularly the timetable. A seventh is the articulation (or lack of it) between the curriculum in the school and the much bigger curriculum that lies beyond the school. An eighth is in the context of the school and its pupils and their origins. A ninth is the relationship of the school with other schools, other educational institutions such as universities, colleges and charities, and with the agencies which fund them and how admissions are arranged. A tenth is the purpose of secondary education and schooling itself.

I have dealt insufficiently with each of these vital factors, all of which powerfully affect each other. But I have understood, which policy-makers have not always done, that they are inter-related cogs. Move one and you affect another. Clearly for the emerging international collegiate to be given practical expression, all ten aspects need to be examined in greater detail. Many of them are addressed elsewhere in this book.

Notes

1   Anthony Gidden's works illustrate graphically and persuasively the rapid changes in our world for which schools ought to prepare their pupils. See also Halpin, 1997, 'Fragmentation into different types of school: diversifying into the past?', in Pring R.E. and Walford G. (eds) *Affirming the Comprehensive Ideal*. London, Falmer Press.

2   H.G. Wells.
3   One example of an incentive that would promote interdependence and collegiality among the grouping of schools would be for the collegiate's results to be published as a whole with each constituent school's funding being dependent on the performance of the weakest. It ought to appeal to those who espouse 'social justice', but who do not quite have the courage to act in their personal decisions on the Tawney assumption that we should want for other people's children what we want for our own.
4   It may be that with the growth of 'education otherwise' the collegiate will offer 'associate pupil' status to those whose parents are embarking on educating their youngsters at home.
5   There are compelling reasons to believe that models of teaching are changing as a result of the learning technologies and as teachers extend their repertoire of techniques in the light of those changes.
6   At present 'summative', 'informative' and 'quantitative' dominate. So too does 'assessments' of the individual pupil's recall and successful handling of information in a terminal examination. All these aspects have their place. But if they dominate, they effect how schools organise and prioritise – to some extent to the detriment of team assessment, collective working and assessment of 'values' and a wider range of 'skills' than most present school life and timetables accommodate. (The 'ASDAN' and GNVQ models undoubtedly consider the repertoire of assessment, but more needs to be done if we are to reflect our changed view of intelligence/talent.)

Tract 25

Extended schools

Phil Street, Chief Executive of Continyou, sees extended schools as an example of ways in which future schools can serve and belong to modern communities in town

The Education Act 2002 contained powers that enabled governing bodies of schools to provide facilities and services that directly benefit pupils, their families and the wider community. This legislation announced the arrival of extended schools.

The extended school is the most ambitious development in education for a generation. Their approach provides exciting new opportunities for raising and sustaining school improvement, for widening participation in learning and for securing for schools a significant role in the renewal of our communities.

The remit of extended schools means that these are institutions fit for the twenty-first century. They embody a recognition that our communities have been totally transformed over the past hundred years and that our schools have to respond. If it were possible to travel through time from the Victorian age, those undertaking that journey would consider themselves fortunate if their arrival point in the twenty-first century was to be one of our schools. This is because they may be able to find certain touchstones and activities within our schools today that were not unfamiliar. However, once the intrepid time traveller set foot outside the confines of the school they would be totally confused. For although over the decades many aspects of schools have altered beyond measure, there remain certain facets that are largely unchanged.

Extended schools acknowledge the facts that people in communities work longer hours, in many households both parents are in employment, the average distance travelled to work is increasing, access to various welfare and personal services is restricted and that learning is the great passport to jobs, satisfaction and well-being.

Extended schools provide the vehicle to respond to many of the demands of modern communities. In essence the extended school offers a longer learning day, a safe and secure environment for child care, a localised and convenient access point to essential services, a handy venue for lifelong learning and a place where people can pursue leisure and cultural activities.

Extended schools are not a simple rehashing of the village college or community school concept. In many respects the village colleges, pioneered in rural Cambridgeshire some 80 years ago and their urban offspring, the community schools of the swinging sixties and seventies, were more than anything about dual use. They were largely a reaction to the perceived under-utilisation of school premises. The village college offered rural adults, starved of recreational opportunities, access to their facilities. The community schools of the towns and inner cities doubled as locations for adult education and leisure centres.

The extended school inherits some of these characteristics, but the big difference between the two models is that they are no longer primarily about creating space for adult learning and recreation. The dominant concept of the extended school is the contribution that their work with the wider community can make to the two, yet inter-related goals, of pupil performance and neighbourhood renewal.

A commitment to addressing pupil achievement is integral to all the activities of the extended school. To illustrate the point take lifelong learning. The extended school seeks to be a centre for adult education. Lifelong learning will be promoted through both traditional courses and training as well as via more innovatory methods. The extended school perceives the value of adult education for its own sake, but recognises the effect it can have upon pupil attainment. The adult learner provides a role model to school students and where that learner is a parent it is likely that their involvement in education will lead to a discernible effect upon a child's performance and attitude in school.

The importance given in extended schools to engaging parents in education is highlighted by the emphasis they place on family learning and parental involvement initiatives. Like the traditional village college or community school the extended school acknowledges the need to make economic use of its facilities. The extended school will want to ensure its buildings are extensively utilised. The particular focus for this use will be upon offering a location for childcare, health care and a venue for other agencies' services. This use of school premises by other agencies will also seek to be linked to pupil performance. Extended schools make the connections to those things such as diet, good health and reduced stress amongst children and their family's impacts on pupil attainment. There is evidence of the links between such things as poor diet, health, domestic violence and low levels of basic adult literacy and pupil performance. Extended schools recognise the inter-connectedness between attainment and health, family problems and emotional well-being.

The experience gained in New York from full service schools is that by co-locating essential services on the school site their take-up is substantially increased. This is largely because of the convenience of providing services in the neighbourhood combined with the fact that parents do not have to find the money to travel to a venue to access a service. Those schools in this country that offer a base for services provided by other agencies report a similar increase in take-up.

Many schools have struggled with finding a role for themselves in neighbourhood renewal. Extended schools go a long way to defining that role. Investigations have revealed that amongst the indicators of a deprived community is the level of resident turnover. It has been revealed that schools can play an important part in reducing that movement. Schools can arrest the rate of turnover because parents value good schools and try to remain close to such schools so that they can ensure a place for their children. Additionally, schools can further add to their value to deprived communities by offering childcare or provision outside the normal school day.

People living in disadvantaged neighbourhoods welcome the provision of breakfast clubs, nurseries, after-school care and out of school hours learning. Such opportunities increase the possibilities for parents to gain employment or participate in training. The offer of out of school hours learning has also had an enormously positive effect. It not only gives parents peace of mind that their children are in a safe and secure environment beyond the normal school day, but out of school hours learning is appreciated by pupils, many of whom indicate that it makes an effective contribution to their performance in school.

In many instances the implications for teachers in out of school hours learning is relatively modest. Adults other than teachers are often recruited to lead the activities. This leads to some extended schools gaining the benefits from extending the learning day without extending the school day.

There are further benefits for adults other than teachers who are recruited to carry out paid work or volunteering in the school. This can improve their chances of gaining paid employment and build their personal confidence.

Another significant contribution extended schools are making to neighbourhood renewal is as a source of advice and guidance. Research has shown that after the GP the school is the second most likely place adults will go for advice on their own problems or circumstances. Schools report that parents often approach headteachers and classroom teachers for advice on their own predicament. Many teachers listen sympathetically and try, when necessary, to refer parents to those better able to deal with their concerns. Extended schools will provide a location for other services that can support adults with specific issues. Those involved in community renewal single out debt as a major factor influencing family's decisions to leave a neighbourhood. Extended schools that offer a venue for a debt counsellor, credit union or by providing financial literacy programmes can assist families tackle this problem, which in turn is likely to make a positive contribution to pupil performance.

There are many positive signs emerging from schools regarding developing as extended schools. Governors, headteachers and classroom teachers easily understand the benefits that can accrue from such an approach. Extended schools do need to adopt a statement of values that embraces the importance of the community dimension and it is crucial that school leadership is fully signed up to the development.

There will be many practical issues to consider. For instance, there is the issue of access to premises. Schools will want to be welcoming, but safe places. It is essential that reception arrangements support access, but guarantees pupil and staff security. There will be matters of wear and tear of equipment, use of premises, suitability of furnishings and building supervision.

Schools will want to ensure that as staff are recruited they understand that they are working in an extended school and the implications of that for staff. Schools will need to be clear about who is their community and have a sense of their needs and requirements. It is virtually certain that schools will need to work in partnership to realise their community's expectations and this will mean that identifying partners and establishing effective working relations will be critical. Few challenge the value of partnerships, but its implementation can be demanding.

A major influence on the degree to which extended schools will be developed will be resources. So many good initiatives have faltered in the absence of adequate resources or have ended when resources have dried up. To a certain extent the key to extended schools will be values and vision, but resources are important in their introduction and maintenance. The Government has made available funding to support development, but expect local education authorities and schools to identify and attract other resources through partnership and promoting activities that will draw down additional resources. The experience of the new community schools in Scotland has been that a multiplier has operated on their core funding. This has meant that they have attracted considerably more funding from other sources than that received from the education department.

Tract 26

Schools for the town

Erik Stein, CSV Project Manager in the London Borough of Barking and Dagenham, explains how young people can use the urban environment as their context for learning and their personal development as active citizens

Inner-city schools, like those in London's East End, exist to help young people make sense of their lives among the pressures, distractions and opportunities of an urban environment. Too often teachers and pupils experience what happens in school as irrelevant to what goes on in the world beyond its gates. Over the past four years a group of schools in Barking and Dagenham has deliberately set out to enable schools to connect the classroom with the community and the curriculum with real life. These schools have shown how a cohesive, community-based approach to the National Curriculum can ensure that learning becomes inclusive, accessible and relevant to all pupils. In doing this they offer a model for urban schools across the country. Much of the work has been stimulated by initiatives designed to promote education for citizenship and to enrich the ethos of the school and the quality of teaching across the school.

The construction of new 'community schools' encourages communication between schools and their communities. The new Jo Richardson Community School in Barking and Dagenham, for example, now hosts a whole range of events and adult education classes every evening. The greater the personal involvement, the greater grows the potential for mutual understanding, motivation and learning.

Eastbury Comprehensive School has successfully built upon this approach with its senior pupils. The school worked with the local Age Concern office to create Wednesday afternoon enrichment activities for sixth form students. Age Concern had been concerned about the mistrust between young people and the elderly community in the area, and saw the link with the school as an opportunity to address the issue. The result was a senior citizens club that meets weekly in the school's state of the art sixth form centre. As well as tea, games and chat, the sixth formers offer the keen visitors the chance to be trained in IT! The club has proved a success, and has gone some way to removing the mutual misconceptions that existed between young and old people.

Schools in towns and cities suffering high levels of social and economic deprivation are bombarded with initiatives to raise standards and widen young people's aspiration. Community-based projects provide a practical platform from which to develop such initiatives. Education Action Zones (EAZs) have proved one source of such education-community partnerships. The Pursuing Excellence Action Zone in Barking and Dagenham focused on three priorities: 1 Improving Partnership; 2 Pupil Transfer, and 3 Social Development. Similarly, the Gateway to Excellence Action Zone paid special attention to ensuring that 'all pupils feel a valued part of their school and that their school can make a difference'. Both programmes led to a number of cross-key stage community activities, such as 'regeneration days', designed to stimulate learning and strengthen trust and social enterprise in local communities.

Effective social action of this kind, when structured for learning, equips young people with the skills and knowledge required in adult life; it also encourages a continuing interest in community activity. For instance, Year 10 pupils at Eastbury School came together around their common interest in environmental issues. Working with the Youth Service and the London School of Hygiene and Tropical Medicine, the pupils took part in a series of epidemiology projects that addressed specific issues in their community. They investigated concerns about the numbers of road traffic accidents in the borough, and looked into the high NO_2 pollution levels in certain areas. The work led to a continuing awareness campaign. The young people were so motivated by being given the opportunity to make a real, visible difference that they requested to undertake their Year 10 work experience at the London School of Hygiene and Tropical Medicine. This was the first time the School took on work-experience pupils. The fact that the project dealt with real-life issues and was linked with higher education proved a powerful stimulus to pupils and staff alike.

Community-based projects need to inform teacher thinking and practice, as well as contributing to young people's learning and motivation. Barking and Dagenham Council recently commissioned three short films entitled *Shifting Public Perceptions*. These were designed to promote equal opportunities and celebrate diversity. The films were shown across the borough at Community Forums, but in order to introduce them to schools, a training day was organised around equalities and diversity in the citizenship curriculum and beyond. This teacher INSET was attended by a local youth group made up of unaccompanied young refugees and asylum seekers who spoke to teachers about their experiences in school, and what they feel schools can do to promote race equality and cohesion. The honest and frank nature of the discussion had a profound influence on the teachers that attended and many of them commented on how it would influence the way equality and diversity is handled within their school, in order to provide a more supportive learning environment for their minority pupils.

There is no doubt that urban schools in the future will gain immensely from creating learning partnership across and beyond their local communities.

Tract 27

Rural schools

Roz Bird, now a Business Development Manager for the Science Park Association (UKSPA), looks at the new ways in which country schools can build on the Cambridgeshire traditions of Henry Morris

The challenge

Rural communities suffer from isolation: they are isolated from the facilities which cities take for granted. The villages and towns of Cambridgeshire are no exception.

People in the Cambridgeshire villages today are more mobile than they were in the 1920s when Henry Morris was developing the first Community College. They do not, however, fully benefit from their proximity to Cambridge. Transport is a constant problem. The average village to village road is narrow and often sided by deep ditches or dykes, a product of the land drainage creating the 'Fenland'. These conditions make driving fairly hazardous even on a good day.

Roads into Cambridge city centre are well used. Commuters sit in long traffic queues each morning attempting their daily journey into work. Meanwhile, once the commuters have left for the day, daily life in the Cambridgeshire villages is characterised by the activities of small companies, of self-employed people working from home or in small business parks, of village retailers and people not employed and not of school age who may use the bus or have a car to enable them to venture out later in the day. At night the commuters' repeat performance clogs the roads and the last bus returns to the depot in the early evening.

People in the villages have the right to access the same educational facilities as those who live in the city. People in small companies or those working from home require access to training courses and the opportunity to meet with other businesses in the area where they work. Adults need to find the courses they want and the space and time they need in their own village or town.

A short while ago educational needs in the villages of Cambridgeshire were clear. Organisations such as the Chamber of Commerce, then the Training and Enterprise Council (now Learning and Skills Council) and Business Link all reported that small companies could not afford to spend time and money travelling to Cambridge (and beyond) to get the sort of training and learning opportunities they needed to help them prosper. Furthermore people living in these isolated communities found it hard to access the right courses in order to achieve the skills they needed to apply for local work.

The response

Five secondary schools at Ely, Linton, Melbourn, Ramsey Abbey with Ailwyn, and Soham have been working since 1998 with a shared vision to meet this need by providing learning *in* the community *for the whole community*. This learning is cost-effective, accessible, and productive. Because these schools are now providing much-needed facilities, people from these communities can reduce their travelling time and access training and development opportunities closer to home.

The schools, with support from their governors and representatives from the Training and Enterprise Council, had to be very clear about why time and energy should be spent creating these facilities and how the results of the work would benefit the school. The headteachers asked themselves these questions:

- Could the school provide the sort of facilities for which people currently commute into Cambridge?
- Could the school's facilities be used at different times to meet the needs of different people?
- Would rural businesses benefit from special membership arrangements in order to access school sports facilities?
- Would adults in the community use the facilities during the day or in the evening for classes and careers advice?
- Could the school set up a business network so that self-employed people working at home and members of small companies could meet?
- Could the school provide training courses, or hire facilities to businesses which would bring funding into the school?
- Could the provision of facilities and services become an economically viable activity for the school?

The schools identified good reasons to turn their vision into reality:

- The schools were already perceived as a focal point for the community.
- The schools already had a relationship with local parents.
- The school buildings could be transformed quite easily into training rooms and meeting rooms, and provide access to catering facilities and

safe car parking at anytime of the day or night. A bit of creative thinking in order to maximise the use of the facilities and the practice of realising assets made sense.

- This new provision appealed to those responsible for the school budget. Revenue from courses and facilities hire would be reinvested in school facilities which would benefit the whole community.
- The profile of the school within the community and within Cambridgeshire would be improved.
- Relationships between the school and the business community would improve as businesses would recognise the business sense in being involved with the school.
- Pupils would benefit from increased contact with local businesses.
- Improved relationship with local businesses would strengthen the ability of the schools to achieve specialist status.

First steps

Facilities

Each centre identified an area of their school which would be suitable as a venue for training; for example, a community room near the reception area of the school and/or with clear access to the car park. Small changes were made to transform the room into a business training suite. These changes included swapping curtains for blinds, painting walls white or cream, repairing and or replacing chairs and tables and investing in some IT equipment such as a small network of computers.

Partnership

In each region of England there exist a Chamber of Commerce, a Learning and Skills Council and a branch of the Small Business Service (named Business Link in Cambridgeshire). These organisations are responsible for two areas of work which have been crucial to the development of Learning Centres in the five schools. Work Force Development involves improving skills that exist within businesses and within the community. Widening Participation is devoted to encouraging everyone (especially the very hardest to reach) to consider taking part in learning opportunities. The schools made sure that these organisations knew about their plans and sought ways to draw on their support.

Marketing

Making people in the community aware of the new facilities available to them is a vital process. Each school has a unique advantage over every other organi- sation in this area as schools have contact with hundreds of local parents every day. The schools made use of these contacts through letters and through the provision of information at parents' evenings and other school events.

Local knowledge and the Chamber of Commerce database were combined to provide a growing database of companies to contact for planned business activities. Setting up a business network and holding regular events gave the schools personal contact with local businesses as well as valuable insight into the local business community's needs.

Initial funding came from the Learning and Skills Council which enabled the schools to pay for changes to facilities and to cover the costs of the first few business network meetings.

The Cambridgeshire model

Today, the schools work together as a network. They have established a brand with local businesses as 'Cambridgeshire Business Training Centres' (CBTCs) and they work in close partnership with the Learning and Skills Council, Business Link and the Chamber of Commerce. The schools have contractual relationships with all of these organisations to achieve Work Force Development and Widening Participation targets. The funding they receive covers use of facilities and often staff time for specific events and training opportunities to be provided using the schools' facilities.

Further funding to sustain the centres has also been gained through 'bid writing', i.e. application for funding. Successful bids have been awarded through TEC Discretionary Funds, Flexible Training Strategies, the European Social Fund and the Local Initiative Fund. Funds have been used to cover marketing costs, to pay for consultants, evaluators and advisers to work with the schools to continue to develop their facilities. Current developments have also seen the enlargement of the network to include a major part of the Fenland area with direct support from Isle College (a Further Education College).

Pupils attending the schools with a training centre can benefit from access to equipment and the opportunity of contact with local businesses. Ely Community College has recently achieved Business Enterprise Specialist Status. The development of the training centre was a key feature of the bid. Local businesses using the centres are being invited to provide young people with information about job opportunities and work placements are being offered.

NVQ training for adults

Adults too may choose to pursue a National Vocational Qualification (NVQ). The schools can register individuals with the accrediting body, provide support and advice to help an individual complete their required 'portfolio of evidence' and provide trained assessors and verifiers to check and award qualifications.

Val Tookey, the CBTC Operation Manager (at Melbourn) believes passionately in the NVQ system: 'It works for people that need a flexible qualification, and it's tailored for the individual. It gives people confidence about their job.'

Lessons for the future

The future is bright for these five school-based centres. Funding from the European Social Fund ended in December 2003 but there are regular opportunities to bid for further funding through the Learning and Skills Council, Job Centre Plus, and The Regional Development Agency. In other regions other organisations may be managing European Social Fund bidding opportunities. The organisations able to do this are known as 'co-financing organisations'.

Funds from successful bids have enabled the schools to build a relationship with the Learning and Skills Council, Business Link and the Chamber of Commerce. In particular, a closer relationship with Business Link offers schools the financial help to meet its own 'Investors in People' and 'Business Inclusion' targets.

Successes so far demonstrate that the schools were correct about the need for these facilities in the local community. The network of five schools and one Further Education College is strengthening its position by undertaking a new round of business planning meetings to secure a strong future for the school-based centres.

To conclude, the message is clear: schools are in a fantastic position to provide a range of suitable learning opportunities throughout the community. Placing the prosperity of the whole community has become an important aspect of the school's agenda. Furthermore, young people can be offered many beneficial insights into business which will enable them to gain greater understanding of career opportunities and a more realistic view of the skills required.

The relationships and the experience gained through this work will inevitably have a positive effect on how new initiatives are implemented by the school and the local community. The work of the Local Strategic Partnership, the activities suggested through the Extended Schools agenda and the work to support the Citizenship agenda will undoubtedly benefit from the contacts, the facilities and the reputation of these proactive schools.

There are a number of Government organisations well placed to enable this to happen all over the country. They are responsible for the Government's education agenda, the Work Force Development agenda and the Widening Participation agenda and because of this they have access to funding and information regarding initiatives which would enable schools all over the country inspired by the example of the five Cambridgeshire schools to take the first steps towards developing this approach.

National Government departments need to recognise the ability of the school to implement its initiatives at local level, and they need to encourage regional and local representatives to liaise with schools. Whilst we wait for this to happen, interested schools can pursue their initial contacts on their own in a bid to respond to the local needs and offer choices and chances for all.

Schools might contact:

The Regional Development Agency, the Government Office for the region, the Learning and Skills Council, the local branch of the Small Business Service, the Chamber of Commerce, the Connexions Service, the Local Education Authority and the Local Strategic Partnership. They should ask them about their Work Force Development targets and their Widening Participation agenda and help them to consider how their school might become involved.

Tract 28

Citizenship schools

Titus Alexander, Editor, makes the connection between education for citizenship and the local constitution of a learning society

Learning changes the world. It increases opportunities and earning power for individuals. It enriches people culturally, economically and socially. Over the last century, science, technology and medicine have transformed our everyday lives. But there are also downsides to learning. Constant change demands new skills and new ways of doing things. Those who are not part of the learning revolution get left behind. The fast moving global economy also wipes out cultures, industries and species, as well as spreading diseases like aids, SARS and tuberculosis. Innovation can have devastating social consequences, as the tragic experiences of asbestos, thalidomide and BSE have shown. Climate change, genetic engineering, cloning, globalisation and many other changes as a result of learning, present this generation with enormous challenges that cannot be solved by the kind of learning which created them.

Rapid changes in technology and the global economy put the Government under pressure to improve skills and education so that the country can raise productivity and compete. Schools are under pressure to raise standards and meet targets. Individuals are under pressure to get better qualifications for jobs in the 'knowledge economy'. The knowledge economy is churning out new technologies which speed up the pace of change, putting the Government under pressure. The fear is that if we don't compete successfully, other people, companies and countries will take our jobs, industries and prosperity. The economy will stagnate, people will get poorer and there will be less money to pay for public services, including schools. A spiral of decline will set in.

There is some truth in this picture, but it obscures a deeper truth about learning, schools and society. The truth is that the world is changing rapidly, and our economy and institutions must respond effectively. The deeper truth is that in order to thrive in the new economy, we must work smarter rather than harder, and learn how to manage change instead of letting it manage us.

This is what citizenship is about. This tract is about how the citizenship curriculum can help schools respond to the challenges of a changing world.

The economy, creativity and citizenship

The economy is not a treadmill. Schools are not cogs in a machine. Teachers are not operatives who 'deliver' a curriculum to pupils who are assessed and graded against a single standard for their ability to drive the treadmill. But it often feels like it, and it often sounds as if politicians and commentators see schools this way.

The fact is that the economy thrives on creativity and diversity, not uniform standards. Our largest industries today – leisure, retail and public services – need different abilities from manufacturing or computing. As a society, we also need people who can care for the very young and very old with compassion and understanding. We need skilled gardeners, chefs, crafts people and entertainers who make life delightful.

But changes in the economy, employment and the environment also need to be managed. If we only teach people technical skills, they depend on others to make decisions about how those skills are used. Technical skills alone will never enable Britain to compete with the skilled workforce of China, India and other countries who harness high technology with low pay to develop their own economies. Producing too much, and damaging the environment in the process, may be worse than being 'uncompetitive'. Learning must therefore include the ability to take part in decisions about how the fruits of science, technology and the economy are used and shared, at a local, national and global level.

Politics is our collective learning process. Political decisions about what and how innovations are used are often more important for our personal potential than individual learning. Some social arrangements increase people's opportunities, while others stunt them. The dramatic differences between North and South Korea, Finland and Estonia, or between Burma and Singapore, are due to their different political systems. At a national level, decisions about investment in industry, public service or how to fund nurseries, schools, universities and vocational education make a difference to millions of people. At a local level, the way in which a council, company or school is run can transform or ruin the lives of every person in it. These are unavoidably political processes.

It is not enough for individuals to learn well to increase their life chances. They need to be able to use their learning in their lives, which depends on the political system. And if they don't like conditions in which they live, they need to be able to take part in the collective learning process of society, through politics, to improve them.

Raising school standards without empowering learners is in danger of increasing social exclusion, because it enables children from disadvantaged backgrounds to get better jobs elsewhere, leaving the least able and most disadvantaged behind. Unless education also empowers people to transform their social and economic circumstances, it becomes a ladder of inequality as well as opportunity.

The only way in which our Government's goals of raising attainment, overcoming social exclusion and increasing economic prosperity can be achieved, is if learning empowers people as citizens, to take an active part in society. In this view, the school is not an institution that produces accredited pupils according to targets in a national plan, like a factory, but a democratic learning community which manages its own affairs.

Citizenship and school improvement

The citizenship curriculum, introduced in 2002, was an important step towards giving all young people the opportunity to learn how to take part in decisions and the political processes which decide what kind of society we live in. But an Ofsted study of how citizenship is being introduced in schools shows that it was mismanaged in more than half and 'well developed' in only one in five (Ofsted 2003).[1] This is partly because citizenship is seen as just a subject, which has to compete for space in an already overcrowded curriculum and lacks the skilled teachers, commitment and leadership to implement it well.

But citizenship itself offers a solution to curriculum overload and low achievement, since many of the skills required for citizenship are needed to involve pupils, parents and staff in school improvement. A comparative study by Derry Hannam showed that schools taking the 'participation and responsible action' elements of the Citizenship Order for significant numbers of students of the full range of academic ability showed attainment in GCSE average point scores (APS) significantly better than would be expected in 'similar schools'. This was confirmed by Ofsted, which judged that the overall GCSE performance compared with similar schools 'were performing consistently better than expected'.[2]

Elements of 'Citizenship Schools'

In order to make learning matter, the school needs a constitution in which every member of the school community is valued, plays a meaningful role, has a say in what happens and takes part in the life of the community to which they belong. In democratic terms, this means having rights, responsibilities and access to decision-making within school, as well as responsibilities in society at large.

Schools like this should be recognised as 'citizenship schools', in which citizenship is practised as well as taught. Schools which become democratic community learning centres could then be recognised as the local foundation of a new 'learning constitution', as a polity in which pupils, parents, staff and local people participate as citizens.

At the very least, a 'citizenship school' should have:

- a written constitution including a statement of aims, values and rights for all members;
- distinct and worthwhile responsibilities for all members;
- democratic processes for parents, pupils, staff and the community to participate in decision-making;
- an active role as 'corporate citizen' in the local community and in relation to the wider world.

These four elements of a citizenship school are briefly outlined below.

A learning constitution

Although schools are usually thought of as a 'service', an institution to 'deliver' a curriculum, values and models of behaviour, they are first of all communities of staff, pupils and others, who manage their affairs according to fairly clear rules. The way in which a school community is run, its ethos, is the most powerful subject on the curriculum, although it is usually 'hidden'. Often it is expressed through the school's statement of aims, development plan, decision-making structure and policies covering almost everything from behaviour to the curriculum. These documents and the legal frameworks governing schools, together with unwritten custom and practice, make up the school's constitution.

The study of effective schools shows that the school community – it's 'constitution' – makes one school better than another. Leadership is only one element of an effective school. How school leadership is developed, appointed, shared and accepted is a crucial element of its constitution, but still only one of many different elements which make up its constitution.

In a democratic society, we ought to ensure that the way in which schools are run is an expression of democratic values and processes. The best kind of school improvement is that which is owned by all its members and continues to develop in response to changing circumstances. Sometimes a school needs an external shock or crisis to tackle serious weaknesses, such as a failed inspection or sharp fall in pupil numbers, but a model of change based on external shocks has many limitations. It would be much better if constant improvement was a product of the way in which the school is run – its constitution.

The following points outline some of the features which should be included in a democratic school constitution.

Learning rights

The language of schooling needs to change from 'have to' and compulsory education, to one of rights. The UN Convention of the Child, which Britain has ratified, includes a number of rights for children as well as a duty to teach children their rights. Understanding and using rights is fundamental to a democratic society. In practice, pupils, parents and even teachers have to do what they are told and follow the rules rather than exercise their rights. Home–school agreements could be used to develop mutual understanding of rights between parents, pupils and school, but in practice they are more often used to tell parents what to do.

The process of drawing up and agreeing a 'bill of rights' for each class and for the school as a whole, involving all members of the school community, is an education in citizenship. Such rights might include the right to learn, to be valued, to have a say in decisions, to be heard, to have a fair hearing, to have access to certain resources and support. Most rights anyone would want are already enshrined in law and the UN Convention of the Child, but are rarely fully expressed or experienced as such by school students. A minimum statement of enforceable rights would be an essential requirement of a citizenship school.

Learning responsibilities

Responsibilities are as important as rights, and in practice opportunities for children and parents to have real responsibilities within school are often limited to doing what they are told. However, a growing number of schools are making sure that each pupil takes responsibility for something within the classroom, the playground and the school calendar.

Other responsibilities which would be an essential requirement of a citizenship school include:

- producing a newsletter;
- conflict resolution or mediation;
- devising and carrying out a project, as in *Changemakers*;
- undertaking research aimed at school improvement;
- involvement in the appointment of teachers, including the head;
- community service;
- a specific responsibility for the natural environment;
- experience of controlling finance.

All of these responsibilities are being exercised by pupils in some schools. The mark of a citizenship school is that all pupils and parents have a clear duty for which they are responsible.

Learning to participate

Citizenship schools would encourage active participation in school life at all levels. Democracy is as much a culture and way of doing things as formal structures, but structures also facilitate cultures and processes.

In particular, citizenship schools would involve pupils in:

- regular **circle time** to develop empathy, relationship skills and personal values;
- **schools council** with elected representatives from each class and a meaningful role in all decision-making;
- **pupil representatives** on the governing body, by adults in primary school and school students at secondary level, and a whole school council or meeting.

For parents, participation would take place through:

- **class meetings** of all parents of children in each class, meeting two or three times a year to discuss the curriculum, concerns about the class and issues affecting the school, as well as to socialise and support the class;
- **parents' councils** consisting of elected representatives from each class;
- **parents' representatives** on the governing body, as at present, and on a whole school council;
- **parents' representatives** on local education committees.

For youth and community groups using the school premises, or group activity in the local area, citizenship schools would have a **community council** through which community facilities and activities would be run.

In addition to the governing body, on which all stakeholders are represented, there is a place for a **whole school council** or **meeting**. Developing the whole school assembly into a forum to receive and approve an annual report, school development plan and amendments to the constitution would give everyone in the school community an opportunity to experience some of the formal arrangements of democratic processes.

Conclusion

This tract attempts to outline the feature which a democratic 'citizenship school' might have. The aim is to ensure that every school member has a real experience of citizenship. In this way, schools would develop as **neighbourhood foundations of the constitution**, a 'polity' in which pupils, parents, staff and local people participate as citizens, not consumers or servants or authorities. This would enable schools to develop as learning organisations, structured round people's needs and capacity for learning. It would enable schools and their members – pupils, parents and staff – to respond more thoughtfully and effectively to the rapidly changing world in which we live.

For further details, see *Citizenship Schools: A Practical Guide*, published by Campaign for Learning/Southgate, The Square, Sandford, Crediton, Devon EX17 4LW (email: info@southgatepublishers.co.uk), £14.95 plus £1.50 p&p.

Notes

1 Ofsted, National Curriculum Citizenship: planning and implementation 2002/03, June 2003, HMI 1606. www.ofsted.gov.uk/publications/docs/3312.pdf
2 *The Impact of Citizenship in Schools.* Derry Hannam (CSV) Reports on, 10 May, 2002.

Tract 29

School of the future

Tony Hinckley, previously Director of the 21st Century Education Project, describes the school of the future

The school of the future, if it is to respond to the needs of our children and grandchildren, will be rooted in human rights, alert to the social and political challenges of the time, and equipped to offer children, young people and older citizens the learning they need to fulfil their lives and participate in society. Here is my vision of how a future school will look.

Developing learning communities

No system should measure success by whether everyone gets the same results. But it must measure its morality by whether they get the same chance.

(David Miliband, School Standards Minister)

The school of the future will develop through the establishment of federated Community Learning Centres (CLCs) where learning opportunities will be accessible 24 hours a day, seven days a week, either physically or via Information Communications Technology. ICT and access will be an entitlement for all the community, and curriculum provision will be rich, varied and relevant to the needs of the learners.

Each federated Community Learning Centre will be a partnership between schools (primary, special and secondary), colleges, further and higher education centres and libraries, and will have its own governing body or management group. Staff in the CLCs will have a wide range of qualifications, experiences and contractual arrangements. Flexible contracts will be an essential feature to enable deployment to meet needs. Most staff will be located at the CLCs whilst others might also be available electronically to provide teaching, tutorial support and counselling. ICT will link the centres to each other and to homes and employers.

Learners of all ages will be able to attend for tutorial work and self-supported study, as well as for formal lessons or training. A wide range of courses and opportunities, combining the academic, vocational and occupational will be offered physically and electronically. However, these labels are, in themselves, an issue in perceived value and simply changing the labels will not change the perceptions (are medicine, law and education vocational or academic?). Re-naming 'vocational' courses as 'applied' courses is like re-naming a ship as a boat. We still know what it is and what it does – and how it compares with an aeroplane. All courses on offer should contain theoretical and practical (even applied) components. We must aim to value the differences and their contribution to society, not rank or rate them.

Attendance at the Community Learning Centres will be based upon age and need rather than on calendar year. Familiar patterns of the school day and year, and the nature of 'a day in school' will change. The length of a term will be based on learning needs of students, not those of pre-industrial agriculture. For older students the concept of a term will rapidly disappear as learning is related to personal targets. Increased flexibility in the nature and timing of assessments will encourage learning flexibility. Assessments will be designed to assist learning and to measure what students can do only when they are ready.

Funding for the centres will come from private and public sources. Public funding will come from Central Government, local government, and Learning and Skills Councils. Private funding will come from those accessing the Community Learning Centres for specific courses and also from sponsors of courses that address local needs.

Community Learning Centres will serve the community beyond the formal educational role. By involving the community in policy and practice, needs will be identified along with views from the provision of labour market intelligence.

A focus on learning

Learning is not compulsory – but neither is survival.

(W. Edwards Deming)

The main role of Community Learning Centres will be to develop in all people the skills and attitudes that will enhance their natural state as learners. Children are born with an insatiable motivation to learn. It is a sadness that the systems in which they grow up slowly but steadily whittle away at this motivation. These 'forces of destruction' exist in schools as much as, or even more than, elsewhere. Therefore, the approaches to learning must open up a wide range of possibilities for young people in particular and not close down potential opportunities. The barriers to learning must be identified and systematically removed if learning is to be seen as natural, valued and cherished, as well as taking place everywhere and at all times.

If learning is defined as a change in the cognitive state of the individual, then the importance of interaction between individuals must be recognised also, for learning best takes place in a communal or collaborative context. There will be a focus on the learners, their attributes and needs, and a paradigm shift from the centrality of the organisation to centrality of the individual learner.

Here rests the concept of a learning society where learning is valued, encouraged and enabled for all. This concept remains a cliché unless strategies are in place to deliver the vision. *All* learning needs to be valued at whatever level and for whatever purpose.

At home

We need to address what is actually happening in homes of today and in the future. Parenting skills are extremely important, as is the importance of the 2 to 4 age range. This will include education that helps prevent unwanted pregnancies, care for the unborn child and early years development. CLCs will help develop parenting skills in order that children's learning can be enhanced at home through play. Recent research (e.g. Linke 2000; Schools Plus Report 2000) indicates that early, positive and regular interaction with parents (e.g. reading, talking, playing) gives children a head start in life – an absence of this interaction cannot be made up later.

We must also address the influence that aspects such as diet plays on the cognitive development of young people. In this area we have, perhaps, only just begun to scratch the surface of understanding the connections between diet, health, environment and the capacity to learn.

The media will play an increasingly important role in the future in offering learning opportunities to families and individuals in their own homes. Interaction and involvement with these developments will be vital for schools in order to define, capitalise on and support learning in the family situation.

At Community Learning Centres

A mind is a fire to be kindled not a vessel to be filled.
(Plutarch AD 46–AD 120)

In the early stages (say, from age 4 to age 14) an agreed common core of curriculum experiences and opportunities will be needed. This will need to be designed to develop the skills and attitudes related to learning and life in general. From age 14 to age 19 young people may learn through self-supported, individualised programmes, with youngsters negotiating what/when/how learning should take place. The potential tension between the need to follow a prescribed curriculum and the personal motivation or desires of the learner will need to be addressed. The curriculum will become an area of negotiation with each learner.

Students as well as teachers will need to understand better the potential of the human brain and the strategies we can adopt to maximise its potential. Emergent work on learning styles, theories of 'multiple intelligences' and learning to learn strategies will need to be embedded, resulting in a shift of emphasis from teaching to learning. We need to investigate further what motivates people to learn and identify and remove the barriers to learning and motivation. Understanding the importance of the emotional state of the learner is vital as is developing the ability to articulate feelings in an assertive but non-threatening manner. The concept of 'high challenge–low threat' as the most productive learning environment must be woven throughout learning situations and programmes.

The use of ICT in enhancing learning and opportunities for learning needs to develop further. Resourcing to ensure entitlement for all will increasingly become an issue, but we are not talking here merely of 'schools of today with more kit', nor of ICT and the 'virtual teacher'. ICT will be used as a tool for collaborative learning across national and international boundaries, guided and facilitated by skilful teachers who will be just some of the players in the learning process in our communities.

In the community

Community Learning Centres will see themselves as leaders of the educational and learning processes, taking the initiative in such areas as the development of family learning opportunities (more than simply learning 'schoolwork' at home). CLCs will ensure that all young people have an entitlement as well as the necessary encouragement and support to achieve their potential. Education must be inclusive of all learners of all ages and backgrounds, of all abilities and disabilities, of all tendencies and beliefs.

We should involve adults, other than teachers, in the learning process and celebrate the achievements and enjoyment of learners, whatever the context and whatever the age. The current Government's scheme, Connexions, suggests one model for some of this involvement. We should utilise the media in a positive manner, both to support learning in a variety of locations and contexts and also in celebrating the achievements and enjoyment of learners.

All learning, in whatever location, at whatever level and for whatever purpose must be valued and offered appropriate recognition and accreditation.

The whole process of socialisation is part of this argument and a multi-agency approach is essential in order to capitalise on the potentials of young people (see Tract 27 and Tract 28). This will extend beyond the school and home into health, housing, social services, industry, commerce, etc.

... and in creating a better society

> The single most important social institution is the place where we hand on our values to the next generation – where we tell our children where we've come from, what ideals we fought for and what we learned on the way. Schools are where we make children our partners in the long and open-ended task of making a more gracious world.
>
> (Dr Jonathan Sachs, Chief Rabbi)

It will be important not to overlook the social, moral and ethical contribution CLCs will continue to make to society. Currently many schools provide the 'social glue' giving structure and certainties to many young people and their families, whereas life is often lacking such structure and is full of uncertainties (but also full of information and, increasingly, access to information without controls). Therefore, parenting skills should be at the forefront. These might include how parents could help their children to learn, supporting literacy, numeracy and information communications technology (ICT), the impact of diet and exercise on learning and behaviour, managing time, personal finance and maximising opportunities.

Community Learning Centres will have to become more flexible to make best use of specialist buildings and facilities, whilst capitalising on the resources and contexts in the various communities in which schools are located. Students will not keep regular hours since such flexibilities will not be compatible with the 8.45–3.30 school day. The 'welfare-dependency' aspect of 'free' school meals, etc. will also need to be considered further.

The Community Learning Centre will lead what is, in effect, a multi-agency approach, i.e. the physical site of the institution contains a range of professionals all working in concert to meet the needs of the young person.

There is currently a clear tension between the roles of schools as experts in curriculum pedagogy and the social roles schools have to play (both implicitly and explicitly). It is part of the business of schools to 'teach' aspects of citizenship and how to cope in modern society. But citizenship should be lived rather than taught. What better way for ensuring young people play their full role in adult democratic processes than through their engagement in real democracy and citizenship activities during their formative years?

Students will need to be encouraged and helped to become active citizens locally, nationally and globally rather than passive subjects. Ensuring the provision of an educational 'bill of rights' for students will be a fundamental part of the social development role of Community Learning Centres. With rights go obligations, and the exercise of these is essential to the development of active citizens.

Part of the social and educational role of Community Learning Centres will involve the development of the autonomous individual. Therefore they will have to consider how to provide learners with the authority to make choices about content, form and direction of their own learning. Learners having more influence and control over their own destiny and mode of operation will inevitably mean teachers having less control than at present. This is a challenge not to be taken lightly. It will require courageous leadership.

Leadership – a vital ingredient

> ... the focus of the education system of the future will have to be on the community ... educational leadership has to switch from institutional improvement to community regeneration.
>
> (John West-Burnham)

Education leaders will provide the inspiration for others to achieve what they might not have imagined possible. As well as leading learning, we must be the leading learners in our organisations and communities and set the necessary personal example to others.

Teachers will not lose their responsibility for curriculum pedagogy. They will need to develop further their professional expertise in the area of leading learning rather than the management of teaching. The management of increasing numbers of 'para-professionals' (e.g. Teaching Assistants) will become the norm. Development of assessment strategies that are diagnostic and management of groups that are not necessarily age related provide other examples of the changes and challenges.

The role of the governors in strategic planning will need to be enhanced, but will they continue to be lay appointees or should a more professional (paid) dimension develop? The nature of the school as a centre for community learning (providing leadership, vision, expertise and resources) will mean an enhanced role for governors, possibly with increased financial implications. Community Learning Centres that operate as 24-hour, 365-days-a-year organisations, will need a different approach to governance in order to fulfil this different role in the community. CLCs will become more community focused – communities will become more involved and engaged.

So what will be different?

What might we see that is different? Imagine the education system of your dreams. How about well motivated, high performing learners, minimal disaffection, excellent attendance; *real* entitlement and access to learning opportunities throughout life no matter where, what or who you are; a curriculum that is relevant to individual needs, flexible and accessible; assessment when ready, designed to help learning? How about joy in work for learners and teachers alike? How about a better society?

Surely we will expect to see improved results in public assessments and exams, at least meeting and, hopefully, exceeding government expectations. In addition increased uptake of learning opportunities and raised self-esteem in learners of all ages will be evident, leading to a better-qualified population and improved employment opportunities for the people. A significant improvement in morale and sense of community well-being and pride in residents and employees nation-wide will ensue, as well as increased participation in social and economic prosperity. Surely, simply, a better society.

Of course we need to be careful not to discard all the good practice that exists in our schools. We mustn't 'throw the baby out with the bathwater' but, to pursue the metaphor, find a 'smarter way of cleaning the baby' – and quickly, because time is against us. We have the intelligence to see what lies very soon before us in terms of social exclusion and unrest. We can't wait for the slow process of natural evolution or for some cataclysmic stimulus to stir us into action. Accelerated evolution is a process that could provide an education system best suited to the needs of learners of all ages in the twenty-first century. Such change needs the vision and courage to take decisive action based on sound theory.

AGENDA FOR CHANGE

Schools of the future should be:

Federated Community Learning Centres (CLCs) where learning opportunities would be accessible 24 hours a day, 7 days a week across the year.

CLCs would be a partnership or college of educational institutions.

Staff would have a range of qualifications, experiences and flexible contractual arrangements.

ICT would link the centres to each other and to homes and employers.

Learners of all ages would be able to attend for tutorial work and self-supported study, as well as for formal lessons or training.

The curriculum would combine the academic, vocational and occupational elements and would match experiential with theoretical learning.

The timetable and length of the term would be flexible and based on learning needs of students.

Assessment would assist learning and measure what students can do only when they are ready.

Funding would come from private and public sources.

CLCs would serve the learning and development needs of the communities they serve and, where possible, their physical design and location would foster strong links between public services, business and community organisations.

Chapter 5

Tomorrow's educators

Letter to a classroom teacher

Dear Teacher,

Our future is in your hands

The time you spend with children can transform their lives. You affirm their sense of themselves and their abilities. You inspire their enthusiasm for learning and for the subjects you teach. You raise their aspirations and open doors. And as a result, you shape the world for generations to come.

In your class today are the artists, builders, cooks, doctors, scientists, teachers, urban planners, visionaries, web designers and whatever else of tomorrow. The inspiration, ideas and information they gain through you is a powerful thread in the fabric of the future. Do not underestimate the importance of what you do.

Of course you do not do it alone. Parents, classroom assistants, other children, members of the community, television, advertisers, pop singers, the Internet, story tellers and many others influence children's learning. But what happens in the classroom is critical. It can be a place where young people switch off from learning, or where they discover something new and important for their lives.

The nature of schools will change dramatically, and with it the role of teachers. Young people will enjoy a growing variety of learning opportunities. Technology will give them access to all the information they can handle. Schools will become collegiate institutions, sharing premises, resources and expertise. But teachers will be even more important. As guides to learning, you will help young people make sense of the world and create their own future as learning citizens. You will take the lead in transforming schools to meet the needs of our children.

Our future is in your hands.

Titus Alexander and John Potter

Tract 30

Honour teachers

Jonathan Sachs, the Chief Rabbi, explains that to defend civilisation we need schools, and that in taking schools seriously we must take teachers seriously

We don't honour teachers enough. We blame schools when they fail, which is rarely. But we don't sing their praises when they succeed. For us as Jews, the greatest leader we ever had was Moses. And what fascinates me is the title we gave him. Moses was a liberator, a lawgiver, a military commander and a prophet. But we call him none of these things. Instead we call him Moshe Rabbenu, Moses our teacher. Because that, for us, is the highest honour. And the reason, I think, is this.

Long ago the Jewish people came to the conclusion that to defend a country you need an army. But to defend a civilisation you need schools. The single most important social institution is the place where we hand on our values to the next generation – where we tell our children where we've come from, what ideals we fought for, and what we learned on the way. Schools are where we make children our partners in the long and open-ended task of making a more gracious world.

And so, from the biblical era to today, Jews became a people whose passion was education, whose greatest love was learning, whose citadels were schools and whose heroes were teachers. Jewish law contains an extraordinary provision. In ancient times there were places set aside as cities of refuge for people needing protection. And the rabbis ruled that if a student has to go there, his teacher has to go with him. Why? Because, in their words, life without a teacher is simply not a life.

Teachers open our eyes to the world. They give us curiosity and confidence. They teach us to ask questions. They connect us to our past and future. They're the guardians of our social heritage. We have lots of heroes today – sportsmen, supermodels, media personalities. They come, they have their 15 minutes of fame, and they go. But the influence of good teachers stays with us. They are the people who really shape our life.

Tract 31

Headteachers as 'lead learners'

Tamsyn Imison, previously headteacher of Hampstead School, spells out the reasons why teachers need to see themselves and be seen by their students as lead learners

An outstanding school must be a true Community of Learners. This requires the headteacher to be a 'lead learner': to have a clear vision of learning, to have a holistic approach to the whole curriculum, to be an orchestrator of learning and while in that role often allowing others to lead, to be actively engaged in their own learning, to overtly value learning and to ensure that important talk is focused on learning. This is between colleagues individually and in varied teams, between colleagues and their students, the parents and the community as well as between students, parents and the community. The school will then become a true learning community with every one a learner. This learning community will be one where people view learning as a transformational collaborative and creative process.

There are ten important ways headteachers can make their school outstanding as learning communities:

1 'Do as I do' is a far more powerful message than 'Do as I tell you'. The head of a school must be a lead professional and a lead authority. This can only happen in our rapidly changing and challenging educational environments if we remember it is critical to nourish and support ourselves as well as the others. Far too often headteachers feel they cannot leave their schools and that money must go to others first rather than themselves. Remember the cabin crew advice to always get your own supply of oxygen before helping others especially children! Rigorous study sharpens the intellect and brings critical insights after structured reflection. Learning with others outside your own school gives you further insights vital to a broad balanced perspective.

2 Then most of a learning headteacher's time has to be focused on supporting colleagues to do the same. Use the Investors in People audit and process to ensure all colleagues – teachers, specialist support teachers, mentors, administration and site staff are all supported in their own individual learning. Spend time every day to go round and talk to colleagues on their own territory and listen to and use their learning experiences.

3 Build a series of teams with colleagues who love learning, who like people, who enjoy working and learning with others, who have no fear that sharing will diminish their own achievements, and who have a zest for their own areas of interest as well as those of others. The sparks that need to pass on enthusiasm as well as skills and sustained effort only comes from those that exhibit this thirst for learning and a collaborative style.

4 Consider greater involvement with your local Higher Education Departments and establish an in-house Masters Programme delivered by known and respected HE colleagues to build in a learning core of staff who will bring rigour and reflection to professional conversations on school and learning improvement. Such a programme quickly builds up a critical mass of 'lead learners' needed for your true learning community.

5 Use Initial Teacher Training as a real opportunity for building in team teaching and in-house research. Make sure colleagues are supported in applying for Research grants. Use the additional colleagues – training teachers as well as their HE tutors together with the in-house teams to provide both time and opportunities for more in-depth school research on learning in and outside the curriculum. At the same time involve your key support teams with all the support teachers and mentors and others in this vital development work.

6 Work to make sure that everyone is very, very positive about every other member of your learning community. Good communities are those where everyone feels truly valued and important and where everyone trusts and is trusted. No one does well easily if they are not valued. The greatest successes are often from the least promising members when given support. Supporting those a little farther behind on their learning journeys will ensure that those further on, move even further while sustaining others. This is well borne out by data on school success where there is a good balance and range of skills and achievements within the school community.

7 Expect and insist that everyone keeps on improving upon their previous best, making sure that the structures and systems in the learning community facilitate this, not prevent it. This means ensuring that all ways forward for any student or adult are open not blocked. It means praise and support, nourishing growth wherever it occurs and that means keen observation systems watching for when people do things well and building upon these. It is not good enough to wait until people fail. However,

it is also critical that it is school policy to allow creative approaches where some setbacks or unexpected consequences are used positively to move forward.

8 Have some ambitious **DIM GOALS – Demanding, Imaginative and Moveable.** Our first of these was that every student would still be excited by and want to continue their own learning journey at the age of 16. After ten years in 1995 we had virtually reached this so that it became the established pattern. This is a more important statistic than most currently included within the league tables but of course if you achieve this the other statistics are good too.

9 Make 'learning' far more up front and have many conversations about what learning is as well as how we learn with every member of the intended learning community. Consider a far greater emphasis on the 'competencies' needed for learning (Valerie Bayliss, 1999, RSA *Opening Minds: education for the 21st Century*). Those schools in the pilot project associated with this are finding student and staff motivation significantly increases as well as those important social and group skills essential for life as well as for good lifelong learning.

10 Work to attain a better balance of the three styles of supporting learning by increasing the use of coaching, and supported independent learning – such as one sees in any group actively involved with new technologies, as well as using group seminars, formal dialogues with Socratic questioning and active participation while reducing the number of didactic instructional lectures and responses. With this approach we found students and staff were able to interrogate concepts as well as facts and have far longer-lasting skills, knowledge and understanding.

This will ensure you are working towards your 'DIM' GOAL where everyone will indeed be a learner within a community of learners in an outstanding school.

Tract 32

Learner-centred teachers

Ruth Deakin-Crick, Director of the Effective Lifelong Learning Inventory (ELLI) Research Programme at Bristol University, explains the essential role of the teacher in tomorrow's world

The rapidly changing world of the early twenty-first century has created new demands of education and therefore of educators.

Traditional teaching methods and outcomes meet our needs no longer. The new knowledge economies, and political, social and cultural realities of life in a global community require people who are educated in very different ways from what we have known hitherto.

We need new learning skills, including the facility to create new knowledge. We must learn *how to learn* and to go on learning throughout life. We must master higher order creative and critical thinking skills. We must also acquire the capacity to cope with personal, professional and social change and to tolerate ambiguity and unpredictability. Emotional and spiritual intelligence are essential attributes along with the ability to communicate effectively with other people and to collaborate on personal and professional tasks.

We need to own and articulate a set of shared core values, and to live our lives in public and in private according to these moral principles. These values are the key elements of effective citizenship for the twenty-first century. This means that values education will be a vital responsibility for tomorrow's educators.

In the knowledge society educators must model what their students are to become, not least because we humans are designed to grow and learn through imitating others. This applies to the most sophisticated levels of learning as well as to simple practical tasks.

The harsh reality of so much of our current schooling, however, is that teachers are still locked into teaching a content driven curriculum, shaped powerfully by external assessment systems. Despite overwhelming evidence that this current system actually *depresses* students' motivation for learning and teachers' ability to teach for learning, the assessment system continues its stranglehold on policy and practice (Harlen and Deakin-Crick 2003).

This state of affairs requires moral courage on the part of those who train and lead teachers as well as teachers themselves. Current practice is damaging our ability to teach and learn. We must discover and promote a radically different understanding of what teaching and learning is about. We must learn to live and to tell a new story about education which has learners and learning at its heart, and whose purpose is to address the full range of human flourishing and becoming.

Our current research is seeking to identify the components of 'the learning genome'. We are searching for the critical factors that release an individual's energy for learning. These factors affect us throughout our lives hence constitute a core feature of lifelong learning. We are already coming to the key conclusion that it is essential we help teachers and their trainers to shift from a teacher-centred to a *learner-centred approach* to education (Deakin-Crick *et al.* 2004a).

The 'learning genome' is complex. Nonetheless, it can be readily understood by pupils, parents and teachers and everyone else involved in learning and teaching. Our 'genome' comprises a mix of dispositions, lived experiences, social relations, values, attitudes and beliefs. These ingredients coalesce to shape the nature of an individual's learning energy. In this way they affect the way we engage with each particular learning opportunity.

Learning, of course, is deeply influenced by the context in which it happens. What teachers do, the quality of the emotional climate of the classroom, assessment practices, school structures, processes, tradition and culture all contribute to an emerging ecology of learning which can inhibit or facilitate learning. Understanding this ecology is essential for teachers of tomorrow.

An individual's learning energy is hard to define, but research indicates that there are a number of dimensions of learning energy which can be recognised, articulated and nurtured within learning communities. These dimensions are the sum of the core qualities, characteristics, dispositions values and attitudes and beliefs that characterise an effective learner.

Findings so far show that there are at least seven dimensions that determine an individual's learning energy. These are:

1   **Growing and learning**. Effective learners know that learning itself is learnable. They believe that, through effort, their minds can get bigger and stronger, just as their bodies can. They see learning as a lifelong process, and gain pleasure and self-esteem from expanding their ability to learn. Growing in learning includes a sense of getting better at learning over time, and of growing and changing and adapting as a learner in the whole of life. There is a sense of history and hope.

2 **Critical curiosity**. Effective learners have a desire to find things out. They like to get below the surface of things and try to find out what is going on. They value 'getting at the truth', and are more likely to adopt 'deep' rather than 'surface' learning strategies.

3 **Meaning making**. Effective learners are on the look-out for links between what they are learning and what they already know. They get pleasure from seeing how things 'fit together'. They like it when they can make sense of new things in terms of their own experience, and when they can see how learning relates to their own concerns. Their questions reflect this orientation towards coherence.

4 **Creativity**. Effective learners are able to look at things in different ways. They like playing with ideas and taking different perspectives, even when they don't quite know where their trains of thought are leading. They are more receptive to hunches and inklings that bubble up into their minds, and make more use of imagination, visual imagery and pictures and diagrams in their learning.

5 **Resilience**. Effective learners like a challenge, and are willing to 'give it a go' even when the outcome and the way to proceed are uncertain. They accept that learning is sometimes hard for everyone, and are not frightened of finding things difficult. They have a high level of 'stickability', and can readily recover from frustration.

6 **Strategic awareness**. More effective learners know more about their own learning. They are interested in becoming more knowledgeable and more aware of themselves as learners. They like trying out different approaches to learning to see what happens. They are more reflective and better at self-evaluation.

7 **Learning relationships/interdependence**. Effective learners are good at managing the balance between being sociable and being private in their learning. They are not completely independent, nor are they dependent. They like to learn with and from others, and to share their difficulties, when it is appropriate. They acknowledge that there are important other people in their families and communities who help them learn, and they draw on the stories of their family and tradition to help them make meaning.

A paradigm shift

Teaching which is focused on stimulating and nurturing learning energy is quite different from teaching which is focused on delivering the content of the curriculum and achieving a set of externally directed outcomes. Tomorrow's educators must consciously shift from being 'curriculum centred' towards being 'learner centred'. This paradigm requires a shift in values as well as in technique. Our research findings show that the core values associated with being learner-centred are values which focus on the quality of relationships, the ethos of the classroom and school, practices associated with dialogue, reflection and a high level of emotional literacy.

Learning relationships are those that are characterised by affirmation, trust and challenge and which create a safe climate in which students are able to take risks, and learn. Modelling and imitation is vital in helping students to become effective learners. Teachers need to be effective learners themselves if they are to help others learn to learn. They must be able to model specific learning practices, values and attitudes for their students. Being learner-centred requires teachers to be able to develop their own professional vision and values for learning. Furthermore, teachers must make their own professional judgements about the particular learning needs of their students at different times, and, therefore, not be completely constrained by external demands and expectations.

Research by McCombs (McCombs 1997a, 1997b) supports these findings. Her work shows that the key indicators of student *learning achievement* are the student's perceptions of the teacher's ability to:

- create positive interpersonal relationships;
- honour student voice;
- stimulate higher order thinking;
- cater for individual differences.

These findings show that teachers need to understand and be skilled in developing learning relationships. These types of qualities are not currently a focus for teacher education as they are in the training of other types of caring professionals. Much is now known, for example, about the nature of relationships in other caring professions such as psychotherapy, which is highly relevant to the learning relationships teachers need to establish in order to be effective (Rogers 1994). This also has implications for teachers' own personal development and learning journeys, which are a necessary corollary to modelling and facilitating learning in others (Deakin-Crick *et al.* 2004b, Deakin-Crick *et al.* 2002).

Our research findings also suggest that teachers need to be equipped with the theoretical and professional resources to make their own judgements on matters of learning. They need enough confidence in their own collaborative judgements to have the courage of their convictions in a context of external accountability, which may mean having to do things differently, or against the grain of usual practice. This will require a greater focus on teachers being comfortable with moving between educational theory and practice as a core professional learning skill. Teacher education must address more than technical competencies.

There are significant implications too, for the structure and process of the curriculum. The ELLI research showed that in order to stimulate particular dimensions of learning energy, such as curiosity, meaning making and creativity, teachers would not necessarily teach a *different* lesson content, but they would be *creative in the ways in which they would present* that content. For example, they might set a lesson up as a learning challenge, as a problem to be solved. They might create a situation where the students discover the content for themselves, rather than just receiving it as a 'given'. To this end there is a wide range of possible strategies in a learning toolkit which can be employed, such as knowledge mapping, concept mapping, use of visual imagery, use of Information and Communications Technologies for scaffolding ideas, self-assessment tools for learning, and so on. At the heart of this is an understanding of the curriculum as a means to an end, rather than an end in itself.

Competence-led curriculum

The RSA Opening Minds Project (James 2002) explored the possibility of developing a new competence-led curriculum framework. It started from a different set of principles about the curriculum – that it should be a means of expressing what students should learn from their education, not a statement of what should be taught to them. It is not defined in terms of the content to be covered, or the subject matter to be mastered. Instead it sets out explicitly what students will need to be able to do and understand once they have worked through it. It is thematic and interdisciplinary in style. Some of the core competencies include understanding how I learn, how to manage information and situations, citizenship skills and values and interpersonal skills.

This approach to the curriculum requires much more creativity on the part of teachers. It is not overly prescribed, and transgresses known subject boundaries. Students need to be able to process and transmit knowledge that, in the multi-media based knowledge economy cuts across established boundaries. Such knowledge is always located in and apprehended by particular cultural meanings and values. The ability to identify, understand and communicate those meanings and values, and to understand how human communities create and interact with knowledge of different sorts is not only a key skill for economic success, but also an essential ingredient for active citizenship.[1] One way of understanding this is to say that meaningful learning happens at the point where three narratives or stories meet. When the story of the learner interacts dynamically with the stories of culture and community and the story of the learning itself, then meaningful learning is taking place. Figure 1 seeks to describe this.

Finally, developing the genetic metaphor a little further, learning can be understood as a double helix (McGettrick B. 2002). One strand of the helix is *learning achievement*. This comprises the outcomes, skills and knowledge that we hope students will acquire through their learning. The other strand of the double helix is the *learning disposition*. This is made up of the values and

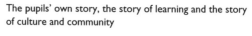

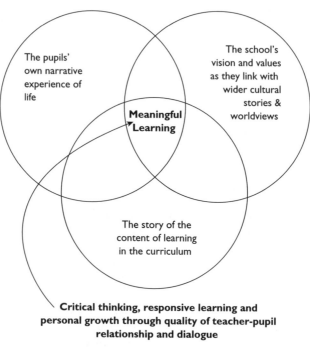

Figure 1 The intersection of three stories.

attitudes and feelings towards learning that students always acquire whether teachers are aware of it or not. In other words, when we teach children mathematics, or French, we teach them to love or to hate mathematics or French at the same time. If learning energy is what flows through the double helix, and the dimensions of learning energy are the links between the two sides of the double helix, then it follows that personal development and learning achievement are inextricably interwoven processes.

The formation of learner/citizens is one of the key tasks of educators, and this takes teacher education well beyond the technical, competency driven agenda, and back into a much richer understanding of education, human interests and knowledge acquisition.

Teacher education faces a challenge. That challenge is to move beyond the domain of the technical interests of management and delivery of the knowledge, understanding and skills of a prescribed curriculum and to give sustained attention to the formation of teachers themselves as professional lifelong learners. It will mean creating schooling structures where there is time for appropriate teacher personal and professional development, and scope for individual and collaborative vision and creativity. Such teachers are likely to be better equipped to nurture and sustain the sorts of communities and cultures of learning which are essential for education for tomorrow's learners.

References

Deakin-Crick, R., Broadfoot, P. and Claxton, G., 2002, *Developing ELLI: The effective lifelong learning profile in practice*. Bristol, Lifelong Learning Foundation.

Deakin-Crick, R., Broadfoot, P. and Claxton, G., 2004a, Developing an effective lifelong learning inventory: the ELLI Project. *Assessment in Education,* forthcoming.

Deakin-Crick, R., Broadfoot, P. and Claxton, G., 2004b, Developing an effective lifelong learning inventory in practice: the ELLI Project, forthcoming.

Harlen, W. and Deakin-Crick, R., 2003, Testing and motivation for learning, *Assessment in Education,* 10 (2), 169–207.

James, L., 2002, *Opening Minds Project Update*. London, Royal Society of Arts.

McCombs, B. L. P., 1997a, Development and Validation of the Learner-Centred Battery: Self-assessment Tools for Teacher Reflection and Professional Development. *The Professional Educator,* 20, 1–20.

McCombs, B. W. J., 1997b, *The Learner Centred Classroom and School*. Jossey-Bass, San Francisco.

McGettrick B., 2002, Transforming School Ethos: Transforming Learning Citizenship Education in Action. Bristol University Graduate School of Education.

Rogers, C., 1994, *Freedom to Learn*. Merrill, Columbus, Ohio.

AGENDA FOR CHANGE

> The only way education is going to change is if the classroom teacher makes it happen.
>
> William Glasser, *The Quality School Teacher*[2]

Classroom teachers are leaders in the learning revolution. Without their skill, passion and persistence schools cannot change. Teachers transform people's lives. But teachers cannot do it alone. They need to be part of a supportive learning community, in which the head, governors, other staff, parents and pupils work together for a common purpose.

Headteachers need to become 'lead learners':

- learning with others outside school;
- enabling *all* staff at school to continue learning;
- using higher education and other institutions to develop in-house programmes for professional and personal development;
- using initial teacher training to build team teaching and research;
- extending learning through coaching, group work and supported independent learning.

Teachers need to develop new learning skills which:

- create positive interpersonal relationships;
- honour student voice;
- stimulate higher order thinking;
- cater for individual differences.

Teachers need to develop and live out shared values which encourage a joy of learning and capacity for citizenship.

Teacher education must combine both educational theory and practice, not just technical competence.

Meaningful learning experiences must be at the heart of teaching.

Notes

1   For a more detailed account of these ideas at undergraduate level see http://www.phil.ncl.ac.uk/

2   Glasser, William, 1993, *The Quality School Teacher*. HarperPerennial, New York.

Chapter 6

Engaging young people

Letter to a young person

Dear Young Person,

Have you noticed that people's attitudes towards you are slowly changing? By people we mean politicians, teachers, and those who run the buses or try to sell you stuff. We agree the changes are slow and some of you may not have noticed them. But the fact is that in some places – particularly in places where decisions are made about consulting pupils, students and young people generally – attitudes are changing. You are increasingly being put at the heart of learning.

Have a read of what your fellow student, Adam Short, has to say (Tract 39). Have a look at the experiences of two headteachers whose work has been transformed by putting pupils at the heart of education (Steve Baker Tract 37). Give thought to what Jane Buckley has to say about young people being at the heart of change (Tract 36) and read about the young people with whom Derry Hannam (Tract 34) has been working.

Finally check out the reasons (below) why more and more people, including Government ministers, are beginning to talk differently about young people and children participating in the decisions that affect your lives.

And don't forget. You too have a role to play in your school and community.

John Potter and Titus Alexander

Tract 33

A checklist for pupil participation

Gill Frances, from the National Children's Bureau, draws attention to key issues in student participation[1]

What is participation?

Participation is when children and young people are involved in decisions that affect their lives. This can be at home or school, through work or leisure, and be informal or formal.

Why should children and young people participate?

Children and young people want to be involved. They want to tell us what they think; they want to be part of the process of creating, building and improving their school. A school culture that encourages participation provides children and young people with knowledge, skills and a positive attitude to citizenship and decision-making.

They are entitled to participate. The United Nations Convention for the Rights of the Child underpins the rights of children and young people to participate. Children have the right to:

> express an opinion and to have that opinion taken into account, in any matter or procedure affecting them (Article 12) to obtain and make known information unless it violates the rights of others (Article 13) to access appropriate information and education especially if it promotes their social, spiritual, moral ill being and physical and mental health (Article 17)

The Education Act (2002) requires pupil's participation in decisions about school life.

There is commitment across all Government Departments to children and young people's participation.

Some benefits

- Bullying drops when peer support activities are developed.[2]
- Effective participation supports school improvement.
- Teachers report[3] that increased participation of pupils improves the school ethos and environment.

Notes

1   Extract from paper on Giving Children and Young People a Voice – Participation and Active Citizenship, by Gill Frances, Association for Citizenship Teaching, 2003.
2   Naylor and Cowie, 1999.
3   Through the National Healthy School Standard (NHSS).

Tract 34

Listen to students

Derry Hannam, Director of the Phoenix Trust, sets out the radical case for listening to students

... if something is interesting you learn very quickly, if you are bored you hardly learn anything ...

(Year 8)

A handful of educational researchers, such as Jean Rudduck and Cedric Cullingford, have for years been listening to the opinions of young people about schools and the curriculum. In the past there has not been very much evidence that their work has had any impact on policy-makers. The attitude of Government to school students has been 'We know best. They are a captive market. Why should we listen to them?'

As a teacher this always seemed to me to be a depressing and stupid attitude. Whether responsible for a classroom or a school my experience has always been that listening to the students pays off. If things were not working well some students usually knew why. If books were going missing from the library somebody knew how it was being done and how to stop it. If there was vandalism in the toilets they knew who was doing it and how to stop them. If the rose bushes were being destroyed by students taking short-cuts to the school buses the students would find a creative solution. Listen, create an environment where students feel that their voice is taken seriously and acted upon, and then involve them in the decision-making and the action, and improvement follows as sure as night follows day.

What seemed obvious, yet hard to communicate to policy-makers, is now at last enshrined in the 'participation and responsible action' element of the citizenship curriculum.

However, these were the easy and obvious issues. Getting beyond this 'housekeeping agenda' to serious listening and acting upon the views of the students with regard to nitty-gritty curriculum and teaching and learning issues has always been more difficult and more contentious. It would once have been regarded as the 'secret garden' nurtured by teachers. No longer. Government, employers, parents have all pulled the walls down and, from the perspective of some teachers, trampled the crops. Not only 'what to grow?' but 'how to grow it?' But, until very recently, there has been no suggestion from Government that the students' viewpoint might also be worth listening to. Is this in the process of changing?

The creation of the Children and Young People's Unit (CYPU) at the Home Office but situated within the DfES is perhaps a good omen. The requirement that all Government departments should create policies for listening to young people is another. And now QCA has commissioned an investigation into how it can best understand the perceptions school students have of the curriculum.

> ... like when we want more books we could tell the government we haven't got enough books ... the government is like a big school council for the whole country ...
>
> (Year 4 councillor)

I have spent some time talking with school students from Years 3 to 13 on just this question. I went to schools that have well-developed policies for listening to the 'students' voice' where young people of all ages have experience of themselves exploring the views of other students. In some cases this involved school student councils and in others 'students-as-researchers' groups. In these schools students had had training and experience of constructing and administering questionnaires, conducting interviews and focus groups, or organising groups of students to keep diaries. In some schools this involved observing lessons while investigating with teachers key issues such as 'What makes a good lesson?' In these schools students believed that not only did their schools listen to their views but also, though to a slightly lesser extent, they did something about them.

I also talked with students in schools that did none of this. These students had far less confidence that their views would be heard or that action might result even if they were. Sadly there are too many such schools as my 80 inspections for Ofsted have made all too clear.

In both groups of schools students thought that it was very important that Government should listen to school students on curriculum issues. The students in the 'listening' schools had more confidence that positive change might follow than those in the schools where there was little or no emphasis on hearing the 'students' voice'. (Though even in the listening schools there was some scepticism especially amongst older students.)

The greatest difference between the students in the two sets of schools was in their ideas about how such information should be gathered. In the 'non-students' voice' schools the preferred method was interviewing by adults who were not part of the school. There was some anxiety about the risk of sharing their true feelings with school staff especially if they were negative and the staff might have a hand in grading their work.

In the 'students' voice schools, by contrast, it was clear from students of all ages that the process of deciding what information to collect and the actual collecting of it should be negotiated with and possibly conducted by the students themselves.

Students also felt strongly that they should be able bring issues to the attention of Government, that the agenda for research should be open to influence by them and that this would show that the Government was 'listening' and genuinely interested in their views.

> ... students-as-researchers should be able to bring issues that students think are important to the attention of the government ... it should not be just one-way ...
>
> (Year 11)

In areas where LEAs were developing networks of student councils or students-as-researchers, students suggested:

> ... all counties should have students' voice conferences like Bedfordshire ... they (government) should have student liaison officers ... they should meet more often than yearly ... like different things come up at different times of the year ...
>
> (Year 11)

Some students believed that there were local, regional and national organisations to represent their views and were upset to discover that this is generally not the case in England:

> ... I was a bit miffed at the level of interaction of school councils and government at the moment ... I didn't think school council finished at an individual school ... I thought there would be something between school councils, it seems a bit pointless otherwise ...
>
> (Year 12)

Students who knew that national school students' organisations existed in many other countries thought that they should have similar opportunities in England:

> ... there should be a small council for school students in each town which would be easy to get to, then a big one for the whole county ... it would be hard to be on a national council while you were still at school, it would be too much travel and time ...

> ... in Norway it is run by people in their gap year ... we should get ideas
> from other countries like in Europe ...
>
> (Year 11s)

Government appears to reject the idea of an organisation run by and for school students that could generate an agenda that comes from and belongs to young people. Such organisations exist elsewhere in Europe, perhaps most impressively in Scandinavia, where they are regularly consulted by governments. They join with parents' and teachers' representatives to review and propose policy. Very often their ideas are implemented.

On a recent visit to England a senior Norwegian educator asked a senior English official 'Why exactly do you not support the idea of a school students' organisation in England? They are so helpful to us in Norway.' The official responded 'I expect Derry Hannam planted that question!' Well, she was partly right, but nonetheless it was a source of genuine puzzlement to the visitor that ministers were unsympathetic to an idea which in his country was at the same time a demonstration of the rights of young people to be heard, an important opportunity for learning in citizenship, and, last but certainly not least, a major contribution to school and improvement and curriculum development.

Perhaps what is currently seen as a 'bridge too far' by ministers could become a 'logical next step' once they start listening to the ideas of the school students?

Tract 35

Talking to a pioneer

Samantha Hoskins interviews Dr Bernard Trafford, Head of Wolverhampton Grammar School and pioneer of student participation

Samantha: Most people think of independent schools as conservative and traditional. In this you appear to buck the trend. What triggered your interest in student participation?

Bernard: Working with Roland Meighan on a M.Ed course at Birmingham University in 1990 opened my eyes and radicalised me. Starting a headship at the same time, I knew a lot needed to change in the school. Going down the democratic path as outlined by Roland seemed the most effective way and one that fitted with my rapidly developing beliefs about how we should treat people (pupils and teachers) in schools.

Samantha: What is the secret of building up this quality of trust between staff and pupils?

Bernard: Leading by example. The head has to lead the way and treat people as he/she would like to be treated. Visible demonstrations of my desire to get down off the pedestal, treat others as equals whose opinions and feelings are valued. Shedding status has a lot to do with it – maybe the most important part of my new book.

Samantha: How did you win your more conservative staff around to this way of thinking?

Bernard: Slowly. By demonstrating successes, that it's better this way – and that there are real benefits for them (e.g. less confrontation, more mutual respect and happy relationships). And some you just won't win over ...

Samantha: What is needed in addition to student democracy?

Bernard: A commitment to self-analysis and self-improvement, to seeking excellence for all. Those are integral parts of democracy, of course.

Samantha: What keeps you going as a reforming head?

Bernard: Zeal, fanaticism. And, yes, I have supporters in the school community as a whole who cheer me up, and naturally some great allies among the staff. There's also a wider network of professional colleagues, including fellow heads who believe in it. I'm lucky – lots of supporters. This is important, because it's a lonely job at times.

Tract 36

Young people at the centre of school change

Jane Buckley, Chief Executive of Changemakers, sets out the social and educational case for putting young people at the heart of education for a change

Learning versus schooling

> Schooling is for horses. It's pre-programmed. It doesn't pay attention to who you are.
>
> (Albanian refugee pupil in London)

In my work with migrant communities and asylum seekers in London, I was powerfully struck by the capacity and eagerness of the migrant young people, many of whom had experienced terrible traumas and were on their own, to learn. They were not disaffected but rather could not access schooling. But they learned so much and so rapidly. Given the inflexible response of so many of the schools to their transition into formal education, one wondered if they would gain anything by entry into school. They were *learning* not being schooled.

In a recent work of Doris Lessing there is a wonderful description of just such learning. Two young children, Mara and Dann, were forced by climatic and consequent economic and personal catastrophe, to leave their home village and migrate to survive. As for many migrants, accessing formal schooling was not a possibility. But, on the move, they had the loving support of an elder who would reflect with them on what they were experiencing each day. 'What did you see today?' A real question with a real dialogue ensuing, each had seen differently and the shared reflection offered further insights and helping in making judgements when facing the next experience. In those circumstances it mattered for survival. Most of us do not face such a sharp need to learn fast and well. Our very survival does not depend on it but we all can learn effectively from experience, others, and ours if such a true dialogue is allowed to take place.

In contrast, when some of the young migrants to London entered school, which they believed to be a real privilege, the experience was at best disappointing, at worst damaging, One Albanian in an East London school emerged after a few weeks saying, 'Schooling is for horses. It's pre-programmed. It doesn't pay attention to who you are. It wants the same outcome for all. Teaching us to know irrelevant things. Like for horses to highstep, jump, trot, canter, perform on command but they always will need that command.' We need to leave school behind and know how to live alone and to keep learning.

Inappropriate for today's world

Today's world requires resilience to cope with frequent change, economic, social and technological; to handle restructured family relations; to live with global awareness and mobility; to tackle fundamental injustices and maldistribution. It all requires personal development of the highest order and the use of multiple intelligences. There is very little comfort zone of certainty or stability.

> First conclusion
>
> We need new learning relationships and new institutions of learning to support them.

New pedagogy: facilitation

One way of building such resilience is to centre the individual in a way that gives some sense of control and power over the turmoil around. Like Mara and Dann and those London asylum seekers, learners need to build their capacity continuously to take stock, emotional and cognitive, not in isolation from others but in a true spirit of interdependence. Knowing how to observe, review, reflect, and then act again, applying the insight gained.

Learning is a centred and centring activity building understanding, knowledge, skills and self-belief (for the individual or the agency), putting the individual in control of self and then influential on others.

> *This happened for Mara and Dann. It can happen for the school population of the UK. But it will require a new pedagogy, a real move away from 1870 and the false authority of the literate few. It happens in much informal education that takes place through youth work and, increasingly, it can happen in schools when experiential and applied learning begins to find equal place with the traditional academic mode. When the engineer enjoys the same status as the lawyer. When we truly value learning not exams.*

Changemakers is a national charity promoting and supporting just such pedagogy. It describes the key educator's role as facilitator and advocates that young people need to take more ownership of the action and learning supported by a facilitator as they move towards independence from the learning establishment. Therefore the educators, if they are serious about the student being a life-long learner, should be in the business of making themselves redundant. The student needs to move from adult control to self-control, to make real choices about what they need and want to learn. Therefore, the adult needs progressively and consciously to move from control to support ... hardly rocket science but where does it happen when predetermined knowledge and information and exams dominate? When outcomes have to be predictable? When you are measured by league tables?

Second conclusion

The student needs to move from adult control to self-control.

In the new citizenship curriculum there is exciting recognition that learning through action is central. Changemakers (CM) is using this to pilot new ways of working in 18 schools through the DfES supported Active Citizens in Schools (ACIS) initiative and simultaneously with 12 others in the Youth Bank in Schools (YBIS) pilot. A central plank of ACIS and YBIS is the formal and informal education systems working together, youth workers and teachers in a joint learning venture; youth workers primarily supporting the action and teachers primarily the reflection and its relevance to the curriculum. Cross-sector training has been offered including teachers, youth workers, Connexions Personal Advisers and other educational support staff. It has been striking how this has broken down the prejudices of each about the other, teachers seen as didactic, inflexible and authoritarian; youth workers as unfocused, purposeless and without boundaries. The real shared interest in young people's learning and development emerges and the institutional constraints that inhibit what each is truly after slip away. Highly productive partnerships are emerging in which this learning and the role of each in supporting it are greatly strengthened. Tensions of course still exist but a joint venture between school and community in experiential and applied learning is growing. It is recognised that action and learning are connected, that much of young people's action takes place out of school and it isn't the sole domain of any one professional.

The central importance of reflection

There is growing recognition that real knowledge is gained from the action, that there is a valid place for experiential learning not just in applying knowledge gained in more traditional ways in the classroom but as a way of acquiring knowledge as well as skills and attributes. The key to it is the *reflection*. Running a tea party for elderly people may be a good voluntary action initiated by the young person 'cos he knows his Gran would like it'. But it becomes citizenship education when the thinking is done about why they want to get together in that way, the cost of living for pensioners and the isolation resulting from poverty, the level of pensions, the lack of private pensions for most manual workers, the implications for the state and the individual and so on. Simple owned action can arouse the interest in real knowledge that the facilitator can enable.

Third conclusion

Reflection about why, how and for what purpose is essential.

A new pedagogy

In the CM model young people lead the action; adults support the learning. The students select action that matters to them, analyse how to achieve it, and acquire the relevant knowledge and skills to make it work. They work with others in a joint venture calling on each person's contribution and learning to value that, engage all the intelligences, and achieve personal and community change. It is a powerful experience and one that calls for a different relationship both at the time and subsequently with the educator. It is hard for either teacher or student to go back, having had a taste of such learning, to the passive classroom model.

Fourth conclusion

The students take reponsibility for their own action and learning.

In the past the practical application of knowledge in vocational education was limited, on the whole, to the least cerebral who would not pursue academic or professional learning. 'Community action is OK for the drop outs. The others haven't time for it.' My first experience of teaching the ROSLA kids: 'Do what you like with them as long as you keep them out of our hair.'

In a new schooling system this false divide has to be avoided. We must move away from the endless English dialectic ... manager/worker, manual/professional, on the one hand/on the other. What about the third hand? Limiting options to two is not the way to build creativity and enterprise that are needed today. Perhaps the introduction of Enterprise Education into the curriculum which is on the cards for 2005 will be another opening for a new approach. Applied learning is valid for all.

As a teacher of sociology I would frequently experience parents' worries that it was changing their child's behaviour, and making them question everything.

This was discomforting for some. My response on many parents' evening was to go home with the unusual feeling that 'this is success'. Where so frequently you knew and struggled with students for whom schooling was experienced as a discrete activity unconnected to life and therefore pointless, this feedback suggested it had engaged the emotions, the values, the spiritual, and the cerebral. It was leading to real learning.

New schools: learning centres

If the arguments above are valid (and much of the writing in this book as well as the testimony of so many young people indicate they are) schools must change to allow and frame such new pedagogy. If schools become such learning centres they will enable the whole community with young people at the heart to:

- network, construct and share opportunities for learning experiences;
- network expertise on all fronts;
- have access to the technology required to acquire, offer and hold information communally;
- use the centre as a pivotal place to reflect on experience and draw out the learning, measuring it where necessary to provide evidence of serious purpose as well as individual progress and growth and acquire qualifications;
- have a centre to develop skills and acquire knowledge needed for action whether civil, economic or social – whether for the individual or for the community;
- share learning with others.

Such centres could provide a fixed point in a sea of change where the reflection and calm we all need to thrive could be enabled, its core purpose continuous learning for all. They could be the centre of the triangle of *personal* development/social or community development and economic development.

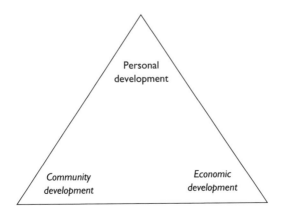

All would come together in a social enterprise supporting the personal development of individuals as earners, learners and citizens. It would enable community involvement that is viable for those least well off; and economic activity that is responsible and sustainable. Some higher education establishments, such as the University of the West of England, do conceive themselves in this way and place themselves at the centre of such a triangle, respecting the context they operate in and supporting their local community through the research and consultancy functions as well as their provision of accessible and demanded courses.

Grabbing the moment/swimming with the tide

It does feel now that there is a critical mass of energy and ideas for a new educational paradigm. There may still be residual fear of the radical but there are also opportunities to head for this vision through careful and mindful engagement with new initiatives such as:

- the most recent techniques for assessment for learning and 'tailor made teaching for each child', Milliband;
- the proposed changes to the 14–19 curriculum and the linking of formal and informal learning and flexible curriculum with ILPs;
- citizenship initiatives which require active participation as a basis for learning;
- youth participation movement and UN Convention on the Rights of the Child. A profound basis for participative democracy and changed school culture;
- the Millennium Volunteers scheme and others for engaging young people in community;
- best value and hear by right reshaping local authority practice.

Holding the vision; young people at the centre

The basis for the arguments above is the need to put the young person at the centre of the educational process. Without their engagement any learning is impossible and coercing interest rarely works. This is so obvious but so frequently ignored.

We have no choice than to put the young person at the centre of his or her own learning.

Tract 37

'All our own work'

Steve Baker, Lead Learner (Principal) of Lipson Community College in Plymouth, describes how his school developed a systemic approach to student involvement

Our school is committed to giving students a key role in its leadership. The vision of the previous writers in this section requires the energy, imagination and quality of relationships that they describe. It also requires good management and a system that will underpin its values. At Lipson College in Plymouth we have drawn on the 'total quality management' theories developed by W. E. Deming. Deming maintained that 95% of all problems are systemic. Rather than 'management by numbers', incentive pay and sub-optimisation, he said we should nourish the individual through intrinsic motivation, self-esteem, dignity, security and 'joy in work'.

In adopting this approach, our school has learned to value and encourage involvement in decision-making at every level. Developing a collaborative student learning culture, including circle time, vertical tutoring, lead learners and peer mediation, was central to this. 'Peer mediators' were initially trained throughout the family of schools to resolve petty disputes. This mediation service has since been extended to a pupil–teacher level and even taken out into the community. Students at each school initially receive training from the Plymouth Mediation Service. The learning is then cascaded to other pupils. Year 8 students, for example, are used to train Year 5 students in primary schools who in turn become trainers themselves.

Lead learners

Students acting as lead learners take real responsibility for their own learning and are trained to support other students' learning. We have a homework club that is run by lead learners. They also work with college productions,

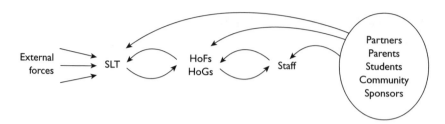

SLT = Senior Leadership Team, HoF = Head of Form, HoG = Head of Guild (House)

Figure 1 Deming's 'life force diagram'.

with training in sound and lighting technology, produce advertising, scenery and props.

Lead learners work with younger students in paired reading programmes and are developing Guild-based Citizenship projects. These are particularly effective in Music, Dance, Drama and ICT. This approach increases student self-esteem and responsibility, concepts at the heart of Deming's 'life force diagram' constructed shortly before his death in 1993 (see Figure 1).

Student voice

All students have a voice through the circle time approach to decision-making and problem-solving. Students are democratically voted on to the College Council, chair the meetings, write up minutes and feed back to their tutor group. 'Circle time' ensures even the youngest pupils have the opportunity to become involved in a free exchange of ideas and opinions. They also vote on issues to be addressed at the council meetings. Ideas are wrapped around fixed themes (agenda items) such as 'successes', 'learning issues', 'environment' and 'events' feed from circle time to the councils through class representatives. There are usually boy and girl representatives from each class at each meeting. This ensures every child gets the chance to participate at some point and is encouraged to plan, to chair, to undertake other executive functions, and to evaluate their work.

In circle time sessions the teacher acts as a facilitator. Deciding when to intervene, or sit back is a real and important skill. Through this process students come to appreciate the true meaning of what it is to be an active member of a community. They help to reshape our core values and learn important lifelong skills that underpin our philosophy. They learn to listen, understand other people's views, think through problems and resolve conflicts. They learn about each other as individuals and develop a true feeling of interdependence. They learn the value of win-win solutions.

Values

Through circle time group members are nurtured by others into living up to values such as kindness, fairness and responsibility. Students and teachers are constantly exposed to human values. They have opportunities to think about and discuss values, gaining experiences that promote empathy. Thus circle time and tutoring encourages us to help students become not only good learners, but good people. It can be used to help students discover their own feelings and strengths and to empathise with others. It is a chance to raise self-esteem if handled sensitively. It is about creating the kind of caring classroom and college that can act as context for community values and attitudes to be developed.

> One of the most exciting developments in modern education goes by the name of cooperative (or collaborative) learning and has children working in small groups. An impressive collection of studies has shown that participation in well-functioning cooperative groups leads students to feel more positive about themselves, about each other, and about the subject they're studying.
>
> (Alfie Kohn)

Collaborative leadership, the development of teams and teamwork, and a broadening out of the perceived hierarchy have all been introduced at Lipson over the last few years: such involvement enhances our enjoyment of work and increases our self-determination and personal autonomy. Collaborative approaches to management have long been articulated. The benefits we get as people from these approaches are broadly similar to those our students can also enjoy if we have the confidence to let go of our rigid control mechanisms.

We also have a well-developed Pastoral system composed of vertical 'Guilds' (Houses). Every student has a personal tutor. The role of the tutor is to 'be there' for his or her tutees. Steven Covey refers to this concept as 'Unconditional love' which means being an advocate for the tutees and nurturing their learning and development.

Own work

Our students are participants in their own learning, rather than passive receivers of packaged knowledge. This has been a key feature of our academic improvements over the past few years. Our philosophy has been 'this is your school'. We put the students at the heart of the college to allow them to develop and grow as individuals with a voice and the realisation that they can make a difference. Significantly, we refer to home work as 'own work'.

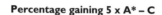

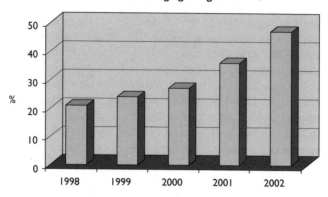

Figure 2 GCSE results.

Our approach has led to real improvements in academic and related work as is clear from Figure 2. Student ownership of learning is certainly not a 'soft option'.

Ofsted inspected our school and were quick to notice the value of an approach based on student leadership. The inspectors reported that:

> Pupils identify with the college aims and purposes and value the oppor-tunities provided for them to be involved in developing the college as a community of learners. Pupils' social development is good. They show respect for other people. Students generally strive to follow the rules of circle time and value the contributions made by their peers. The system of school councils for each year group, circle time and student mediators ensure that matters causing dispute or distress to students are quickly raised and effectively dealt with. It provides an excellent forum where students exercise a high level of responsibility and initiative.

Schools are about people. At Lipson we are very much a 'family' of caring individuals. Ultimately, we are about helping our students realise their human potential, in every sense. We are also about enabling each of us, as teachers, to achieve joy in work. We therefore aim to foster self-esteem, dignity and security amongst all the members of our Community College.

Tract 38

Pupils as mentors

Ann Nelson, Associate Inspector for Citizenship and PSHE in Durham LEA, describes the pioneering student mentoring programme that she set up when teaching at Tanfield School

The Question: Why did you decide to become a mentor?
Three pupils answer
'I knew what it was like when you start a new school'
'It sounded like a good scheme'
'I like to work with younger people. I thought I could make a difference.'

Tanfield School is a semi-rural 11–16 comprehensive school with a population of 595 pupils in the north-west of County Durham. It has a varied catchment area, and pupils are drawn from a wide range of socioeconomic groups. The school has a tradition of peer led activities, and it was agreed further to develop these activities as part of an entitlement in active citizenship. At the heart of the initiative was a mentoring programme that involved *every pupil* as either a mentor or a mentee. This was seen to be part of the school improvement agenda.

My own experience of peer led education in schools was widened during my work as school co-ordinator for the CSV Lighthouse Schools Project from 1997 to 2000. The International School Effectiveness and Improvement Centre (ISEIC) at the London Institute for Education evaluated the project[1] and found that the experience of active citizenship enhances learning and improves personal and social development. It was also stressed that the emphasis on active, experiential and reflective practice is a significant contributory factor in improving progress in students' learning and attainment.

First phase

A peer mentoring scheme was introduced into the school to strengthen existing links between the secondary school and its feeder primary schools and to ease the transition of pupils between the primary and secondary schools. The secondary aim of this citizenship project was to improve the key skills of the older pupils which would have a direct effect on their learning.

The decision was taken to involve Year 10 students to work with pupils in Year 7 during the academic year 1999–2000. The mentors were to be selected from volunteers to the scheme by the writer, after consultation with the head of year. The mentees were identified by liaising with staff from the feeder primary schools.

A match between the older and the younger pupils was made using three criteria: the mentor/mentee pairs should share the same:

- feeder primary school;
- gender;
- choice of hobbies and pastimes.

The aims of the initiative were to:

1   Strengthen existing links between the secondary school and the feeder primary schools and ease the transition between primary school into secondary school.
2   Develop the self-confidence of the younger pupils by increasing their friendship groups to include pupils in the upper school who would give them the emotional support which should improve their learning.
3   Develop the self-confidence, sense of esteem, interpersonal skills and self-motivation of the older pupils with the expectation that they would have a greater responsibility for their own learning which would lead to their self-improvement.
4   Break down the barriers between the key stages and so improve the ethos of the school.

The scheme was introduced to the pupils towards the end of Year 9 during Art lessons. Thirty pupils volunteered to undergo training as potential mentors.

A successful bid to Durham County Health Promotions provided adequate funding for two half-day workshops, to be led by a professional consultant.

Conclusions of the first phase of the scheme

The results for both mentors and mentees were encouraging. Three mentors were questioned in depth about their experience. Each student mentor had positive reasons to join the programme. Debra volunteered to become a mentor as she could remember what it was like when she started a new school. Heather thought it sounded like a good scheme. Stephen had decided to become a mentor because he wanted to help and look after younger people in the school and he thought he could make a difference.

Rebecca

Rebecca, the younger pupil was pleased when she was told that she was to have a mentor. She felt that having an older friend in the school had made her less anxious about her move into her new school. She thought that having a mentor with similar hobbies was a good idea because it gave them something to talk about when they first met. Rebecca's mentor helped her when she first came into the secondary school, especially when she could not find her classrooms. She felt that having a mentor in the school has made her more confident, and she also thought the scheme should continue because mentees had received a great deal of help from their mentors. She thought the scheme would improve if the mentors meet with their mentees more frequently. Rebecca felt that she had gained a great deal from having a mentor and felt that in the future she would like to help a younger pupil by becoming a mentor.

Two mentors, however, considered the criteria for joining the scheme were unnecessary, although one thought they offered a helpful starting point.

All three felt that they had helped their mentees during their first year in school. All three also felt that their own learning had been improved during the project. They believed that their literacy (communication) skills were improved and they were better able to resolve problems.

The mentors suggested some improvements to the scheme. The initial meeting between mentor and mentee should take place earlier in order to build a relationship between mentor and mentee prior to the move from primary to secondary school.

The second and third phases of the scheme

The scheme was extended in its second year. Towards the end of the first year a small group of Year 10 mentors spoke to pupils during a Year 9 assembly. They described their training and work as mentors and highlighted the benefits of the scheme to themselves. The Year 9 pupils were invited to volunteer for training as mentors. This resulted in almost 60 Year 9 pupils being prepared for their role as mentors.

The training for the new mentors followed the style of that in the previous year. However, the specialist training was now provided by the county's psychological service who were keen to work with schools who were looking to increase peer led anti-bullying strategies.

In the third year, we took the bold and significant step of enlarging the scheme to include every pupil in the school as a mentor or a mentee. Mentoring had come of age and was now an entitlement designed to enrich and support the life and learning of every young person in the school and every child who expected to attend Tanfield on leaving primary school. Mentoring of this kind can and should be an entitlement in every future school.

Note

1   The evaluation was carried out by Lynne Gerlach (1999).

Tract 39

Engaging young people in real learning

Adam Short, previously a student at Tanfield School (Tract 38), describes how he discovered new ways of learning and developed a radical vision of student participation

I realised that all my new insights, skills, understanding and knowledge had come through practical experience and reflection. The five years I spent between 1994 and 1999 were probably some of the most challenging, fun, cruel, exciting and inspiring times I will experience in my life. It was of course the time I spent at secondary school, and it was of course as the words suggest and our memories affirm, a time of being young, with all the baggage such a time brings.

On the whole I remember school to be a good experience, though as a moderate academic performer and supposedly well-behaved student, I walked the halls and corridors with relative ease. What made my experience of school different and more rewarding, were the opportunities that were available to have different learning experiences, by placing the learning outcomes of the formal lesson in a plethora of new environments.

The school's ethos of community involvement, and its active role in strengthening the ties with those beyond the school gates, allowed the creation of new learning spaces. In Year 7 Art, formal links were made with a Special Needs school in the local area. Every week both classes met, taking it in turns every other week to host the lesson. The idea was that this new enlarged group worked together over one term on a joint project. The usual art teaching went on as normal, shared by the art teachers of both the schools, but there was now an opportunity for the student to learn *socially*. We learnt to socialise and work with other young people, which normally would not happen, and subtly to develop a raft of interpersonal skills.

The results for me personally included skills development and progress in art itself. It provided motivation for myself and for many others in the group, as we were seduced every Tuesday morning by a different teaching environment, where the teachers' role shifted from the didactic style, where they led and planned my learning experience, to one where more responsibility was placed on me. This allowed us students to be at the centre of our learning experience. A more visible result of the group's work was an enormous mural of Henri Rousseau's *Tiger in a Tropical Storm (Surprised!)*, which was shown with pride in both schools.

The subsequent recognition for this work as a model of best practice opened up new opportunities for those schools involved. In 1997 Tanfield School was asked to become a *Lighthouse School* by CSV[1] under their small pilot of eight schools across Britain. The group of schools visited Colorado in October 1998, and I was a participant. The intention was to research how schools in Fort Collins, Colorado, built active community involvement by their students into curriculum time. I spent time with students on community projects, such as the Food Distribution centre and the 'To School' project based in a Hispanic community.

The work undertaken both in America and in the UK provided me with unique experiences which helped to develop skills, provided me with a new perspective on how I saw the world and fuelled my imagination and aspirations. As well as bringing back to the local community and school ideas we had learnt in America, such as Make a Difference Day, a peer mediation scheme and a profound motivation to do more, these experiences provided me with an opportunity to view learning differently.

I realised that all my new insights, skills, understanding and knowledge had come through practical experience and reflection. I had discovered that my learning was not confined to the classroom. I could learn a great deal through a wide variety of experiences, with myself directing the whole process.

Using this acknowledgement of what I think is my learning style, I became more active in things like the school council, being a reporter for the school newspaper and having the role of prefect. I also got more involved with the work of Changemakers,[2] to encourage other young people to access the experiences I had gained so much from.

I feel my positive accounts, however, elude the greater truth about my experience and subsequent feelings about the role of education and school. I would say for the majority of those leaving school today, this is unfortunately not the account most would be in a position to give. I hope that through the emergence of citizenship education in schools and the debate about education, which is intensifying, there will follow changes, which will allow more young people to benefit from a different view of the role of school.

In conclusion I ask the reader two questions and offer an attempt at an answer to each:

• How do you distinguish an educated person from one who is not?

An educated person will act and relate differently from others, not because she has had more experience or knows more information, facts and figures but because she will be a thoughtful actor, wise enough to know what she doesn't know and can't do and aware enough that she will recognise who does and can. A really educated person is humble and knows there is always more to learn.

- How do we build schools to develop educated people?

We acknowledge what we know about how people learn. We trust young people (the learner) and affirm their experiences, helping them make sense of them. We have a dream but also have a plan to achieve it (Luther King). We take advantage of the opportunities new initiatives offer but always know why or when to reject them. We have the courage to innovate and learn from our attempts. Above all we are clear in our inner self of what we are seeking and dare to lead with a vision of helping all to be real learners.

Adam Short is the first young trustee of Changemakers and regularly represents the Changemakers approach at national seminars and conventions as policy-makers seek to understand how best to reach and engage young people.

Notes

1   CSV (Community Service Volunteers) promotes citizenship education through community involvement in schools, colleges and universities. The *Lighthouse Schools* initiative promoted demonstration projects in active citizenship and involved active partnerships with schools in the USA. (Tract 26, Erik Stein.)
2   *Changemakers*, initially set up in association with CSV, works with schools and youth organisations to enable young people to design, manage and review projects and activities that promote social change. (See Tract 36, Jane Buckley.)

AGENDA FOR CHANGE

> We have no choice than to put the young person at the centre of his or her own learning.
>
> (Jane Buckley, Chief Executive, Changemakers)

Awareness

Policy-makers, governors, educators, parents and young people need to know that:

- **Children and young people** have the right to participate under the United Nations Convention for the Rights of the Child and the provisions of the Education Act (2002).
- **Evidence** shows that pupil participation can:
  - reduce bullying and improve behaviour;
  - raise standards;
  - enrich the school ethos.

Pedagogy

Good teaching *requires* student participation. This requires:

- new learning relationships and new institutions to support them;
- reflective learners asking Why? How? and For what purpose?;
- students moving from adult to *self-control*.

Systems

Effective student participation requires structures that nourish collaborative learning. For example:

- circle time;
- a student council at class, school and community levels;
- vertical tutoring;
- lead learners;
- peer mediation;
- peer education/tutoring and mentoring;
- students as researchers.

National Student Association

Student participation calls for a national organisation run by and for school students to generate an agenda that comes from and belongs to young people.

> I realised ... I could learn a great deal through a wide variety of experiences, with myself directing the whole process.
>
> (Adam Short, Student)

Chapter 7

A manifesto of learning for change

Manifesto: Education for change

Titus Alexander and John Potter

The challenge for schools

We live at a critical time. Humanity has acquired immense knowledge, skills and power. We have created global communication networks and markets which connect people everywhere. We are changing our economy, technology and society faster than ever. We survived a traumatic century of two world wars, cold war confrontation and the threat of nuclear annihilation. We enter a new century under the shadow of climate change, terrorism and shocking inequality. While the West has over £50 a day per person, half the world has less than £4 a day per person in real terms. In a world of plenty, poverty kills over 23,000 children every day. Over 150 million children go hungry. And within 25 years, when today's children are in their prime, some three billion more people will share this planet. Climate change may bring devastating floods, droughts and mass migrations. Wars may be fought for food, land and water. At no other time in history have people faced such challenges.

Education is part of the driving force of change, giving people skills and knowledge to make things better, faster and more powerful. So powerful that many feel the world is out of control. So fast that billions of people are left behind. So much better and more productive that hundreds of millions are being thrown off the land into unemployment or sweatshops in sprawling shanty towns of megacities in the majority world. Education, therefore, also has to enable people to understand what is happening and learn how to direct change, so that together we create a world that works for all.

If our education system is unable to equip people to address the many challenging issues facing them, from the local to global, then the future is bleak, because they will surely engulf humanity, as they almost did during the last century.

This manifesto aims to encourage everyone involved in education to transform schools into holistic centres of lifelong learning so that young people can meet the challenges of the coming century with confidence.

This is a manifesto for learning, so it does not dictate answers, like the traditionalists or functionalists who think they know best. It brings together key recommendations from contributors to this book as a basis for reflection, planning and action. And it concludes with one hundred and one questions which, we hope, will help unlock the potential within ourselves, our schools, our neighbourhood and our world for everyone to live a joyful, worthwhile life.

We work for an education system in which:

1   **Everyone** encourages learning as a means of personal and collective growth.
2   **Young people** are part of the solution, not the problem.
3   **Parents** lay the foundations for learning in their children's lives.
4   **Teachers** and teacher education inspire learning.
5   **Heads and senior staff** become 'lead learners'.
6   **School governors** are the 'grassroots government of education'.
7   We are **partners in lifelong learning,** including public services and other providers.
8   **Policy-makers** develop an equitable, accessible and holistic framework for schools to meet the challenges of change.

The eight steps in close-up

We work for an education system in which:

1 Everyone encourages learning as a means of personal and collective growth

The purpose of education is to enable people to flourish:

- with love, care and compassion;
- deepening their understanding, knowledge and skills;
- valuing themselves and others;
- taking responsibility for themselves, others and the environment;
- appreciating and creating beauty;
- and living according to the values of truth, honesty, fairness and justice;
- as citizens of the UK, Europe and the world.

This can be achieved by:

- reducing the risks and barriers faced by some children;
- creating human scale learning environments;
- multiplying opportunities for each child to develop their unique talents, within and beyond school, in nature and the city;
- making meaningful learning experiences at the heart of teaching;
- giving every child the attention and support they need to achieve their potential;

- developing a holistic approach to education at all levels, which 'unlocks the mind and opens the heart';
- enabling *all* staff and other adults to offer their skills and passions for pupils to learn.

2 Young people are part of the solution, not the problem

Pupils take an active part in school life ways that:

- develops a passion for learning;
- encourages responsibility for what and how they learn;
- gives them a real say in decisions through class and student councils;
- develops a sense of responsibility, autonomy and community;
- connects them with nature and the living world;
- fosters self-esteem, dignity, equality and security;
- reduces bullying and improves behaviour;
- raises standards of achievement;
- enriches the school ethos;
- enables them to become lifelong learners.

3 Parents lay the foundations for learning in their children's lives

Parents' relationship with their children enables them to:

- grow, test themselves, stumble and flourish with confidence;
- share what they know and can do;
- develop values that can match the demands of life today;
- get to grips with the wider world;
- create a sense and purpose to their lives;
- know that they are loved.

Parents are supported as their children's first and most enduring educators. Schools work with parents as partners in their children's education by:

- creating relationships of mutual respect and honesty with children, parents, carers and families;
- enabling parents to understand the importance of their role as educators and what that means in practice;
- creating a positive, welcoming first impression to make starting school a magical moment for each child;
- using home visiting to listen to parents' hopes and fears, and offer practical support;
- addressing parents' concerns early, frankly and empathetically;

- ensuring that parents have the information and support they need, for parenting as well as learning;
- giving clear, accessible information about what children are learning and how parents can help; about policies, resources and responsibilities; and the importance of parents;
- providing feedback to children and parents on how the child is doing and what she needs;
- fostering a community among parents and involve them in the life of the school;
- involving parents in making policies and decisions;
- holding regular 'class meetings' of all parents in each class or form, once a term, to create a forum for discussion and deeper relationships among parents. These meetings can raise concerns, propose initiatives, discuss policies or elect representatives to a Parents' Association;
- working with other agencies to offer support parenting and learning beyond school.

4 Teachers and teacher education inspire learning

1 Classroom teachers

- are leaders in the learning revolution;
- transform people's lives;
- create positive interpersonal relationships.

2 Teachers acquire learning skills which:

- are rooted in relationships with pupils;
- apply new insights into learning and how the brain works;
- develop a wide range of learning methods, including story, performance, projects and e-learning;
- actively promote 'learning to learn' as an approach and set of skills;
- develop the five Rs of lifelong learning: Readiness, Resourcefulness, Resilience, Remembering, Reflectiveness;
- honour the student voice through encouraging *reflective learners to ask Why? How?* and *For what purpose?*;
- stimulate higher order thinking;
- cater for individual differences;
- promote assessment *for* learning that:
  - provides effective feedback;
  - actively involves pupils in assessing their own progress;
  - is used by teachers to improve learning;
  - records and celebrates achievement, and increases motivation;
  - helps students understand themselves as autonomous learners.

5 Heads and senior staff become 'lead learners'

Head teachers and senior staff:

- learn with others outside school;
- enable *all* staff at school to continue learning;
- use higher education and other institutions to develop in-house programmes for professional and personal development;
- use initial teacher training to build team teaching and research;
- extend learning to all staff through coaching, group work and supported independent learning.

6 School governors are the
'grassroots government of education'

School governors ensure that their school develops its policy and practice to:

- **enable parents** to participate in *learning to learn* courses and activities;
- **nourish collaborative learning** through circle time, student councils, vertical tutoring, lead learners, peer mediation, peer education, and pupil research projects;
- **create a learning environment** using display, music, resources, new technologies and the school grounds;
- **provide pupils** with drinking water, exercise and meditation;
- **give pupils opportunities** to develop the habit of responsibility and freedom;
- **enable pupils to develop creativity** and a moral sensitivity of caring;
- **promote self-esteem,** including circle time, one-to-one listening, games and celebrations;
- **foster emotional maturity** and security for children and adults, through opportunities for reflection, speaking and listening in which personal experience and identity is valued;
- **be inclusive** and value everyone and their differences;
- **create a curriculum as a statement of values, skills and knowledge** (in that order) as a guide for schools rather than as a prescription;
- **develop a curriculum framework** that helps young people nurture the skills and competencies they will need to make sense of life's complex uncertainties, using content (subjects) as the context;
- **include a range of skills** including thinking skills, enterprise education, financial literacy, key skills, sustainable development and broader work-related 'learning for all';
- **place citizenship education** explicitly at the heart of the curriculum;
- **use the playground and nature** as an outdoor classroom;
- **support projects and activities across subject boundaries;**

- **free the timetable** to support extended activity in citizenship, art or work-related learning to develop a more inclusive and multi-faceted approach.

7 Public services and enterprise are partners in lifelong learning

The extended schools initiative offers a starting point for strategic partnerships between schools, public services and local firms. Effective partnerships are those which:

- **involve public services** – including social services, health, libraries, transport and other providers – in working with Community Learning Centres (CLCs);
- **offer opportunities for** learning, enterprise and sustainable development which benefit the whole community;
- **plan, design and provide facilities** that will effectively accommodate such partnerships and integrated services;
- **integrate lifelong learning into strategic planning** and service provision at all levels.

8 Local and national government creates a holistic framework for schools

Effective policies are those through which local and national policy-makers:

- create a coherent, comprehensive and flexible framework of policy and resources to enable all schools to focus their energies and resources on children's learning for life;
- give schools and communities greater control over how they integrate and apply national initiatives and policies;
- move *beyond* targets and school improvement to models of school *transformation*;
- promote a coherent examinations framework that embraces academic, vocational, personal and civic education on the lines proposed by the Tomlinson Report;
- ensure *equal access* for *all* children to the resources invested in public education;
- recognise children and young people's right to participate under the United Nations Convention for the Rights of the Child and the provisions of the Education Act (2002);
- support parents as a child's most enduring educators and families as places of learning;
- encourage schools and young people to understand and engage with the challenges of sustainable development in a rapidly changing complex world.

All schools become **citizenship schools** as the constitutional foundations of a democratic learning society, giving young people and members of the school community responsibility to participate in decision-making through circle time, class meetings, student councils, conflict resolution, mediation, peer education, project learning and other appropriate means.

Schools become *Federated Community Learning Centres/Colleges* where:

1 **Learning opportunities** are accessible 24 hours a day, 7 days a week across the year.
2 **A partnership** ('College') exists between educational institutions and other community partners (see 7 above).
3 **Staffs** have a range of qualifications, experiences and flexible contractual arrangements.
4 **ICT** links the centres to each other and to homes, employers and the wider world.
5 **Learners** of all ages are to attend for tutorial work and self-supported study, as well as for formal lessons or training.
6 **The curriculum** combines the academic, vocational and occupational elements and matches experiential with theoretical learning.
7 **The timetable** and length of the term are flexible and based on learning needs of students.
8 **Assessment** assists learning and measures what students can do only when they are ready.
9 **Funding** comes from private and public sources.
10 **Community learning and development needs** are met.
11 **The physical design and location** foster links between public services, business, community organisations and the natural environment.
12 **Inspection** is an independent, external system of monitoring and support for systematic self-evaluation of school development.

One hundred and one questions for transforming schools

> *A caterpillar does not become a butterfly by sticking on wings.*
> *It has to go through a process of transformation.*

Learning is about finding answers to questions and solutions to problems, whether about the meaning of life or how to play football (which for some people is the same thing).

This book offers many answers to questions about how we teach our children to learn. But the answers which really matter are the ones which you and the people around you find for the children in your lives.

Questions are tools for transformation, keys to unlock learning. The following questions are intended for members of the school community to start the process of transformation. Each question, or cluster of questions, aims to encourage people to reflect; to share ideas, feelings and experiences; and to clarify what they want to do to transform their school.

They are intended to create a community of inquiry, learning and action. It may be best if people can answer them for themselves and then share their answers to come to a collective view as a basis for action. They can be discussed by groups of pupils, parents, staff, governors or local people; as part of the school development process, assembly, lessons or scheduled meetings of the student council, governing body, staff, or parents association; or part of a special school transformation process. They may be put on posters, produced as leaflets, or used for surveys and projects. Use them sparingly, over a period of weeks or months – perhaps one a day for a year. The main thing is to create time and space for people to think, listen to each other, discuss, decide and then act together to transform learning and their school. You choose when its time to trigger change.

1   What are your most memorable learning experiences?
2   What made them so memorable?
3   How can your school create more memorable learning for all?
4   What are the most important things that you know and that you can do?
5   How and where did you learn them?
6   How can school enable people learn what is important?
7   What do you want to be doing in 10, 20 and 30 years time?
8   What do you need to know and be able to do in order to do it?
9   How can school help you to learn it?
10   How does the school enable people to learn how to learn?
11   In how many different ways does your school enable learning?
12   How many other ways of learning can you think of?
13   Where and how could people use them at your school?
14   How do you know how effective each lesson or learning activity has been?
15   How does the school use feedback from learning to improve?
16   How do pupils set their own goals for learning?
17   How do pupils monitor and evaluate their own progress in learning?
18   How do pupils celebrate achievement in learning and in life?
19   How do pupils get help and support when they find life or learning difficult?
20   How are pupils involved in evaluating lessons and learning?
21   How do teachers feel about pupils evaluating lessons?
22   What else can be done to improve feedback from learners to teachers?
23   How does the school use its buildings, grounds and wider environment as a resource for learning?

24 How could the school make better use of its surroundings as a resource for learning?

25 How could the school grounds be improved as a place to be, learn and play?

26 How does your school learn about and engage with the wider world beyond school, across the UK, Europe and the globe?

27 What are the main challenges facing pupils and parents in their daily lives?

28 What challenges will pupils face after leaving school?

29 How can the school equip people to face these challenges successfully?

30 What are the main challenges facing the world today?

31 What can the school do to enable people to understand and take account of these challenges in how they live their lives?

32 What do you like best about your school?

33 What could be done to make it even better?

34 If you could improve one thing about your school, what would it be?

35 What are your responsibilities as a school member?

36 What do you like best about having responsibilities?

37 What do you like least?

38 What would help you to enjoy taking more responsibility?

39 What do you want from school?

40 What can you give the school community?

41 What is your school for?

42 Which of these purposes do you support, and which do you disagree with?

43 How could your school do more of what you want it to do?

44 How do you know if your school is doing what you want it to do?

45 What could you teach other people at school?

46 When and how could you teach it?

47 Who could help you do it?

48 How does the school treat the most vulnerable, difficult or disadvantaged members of its society?

49 What support and encouragement could you give to one other member of the school community on a regular basis?

50 When and how will you do it?

51 How will the other person show and tell you what is most helpful to them?

52 How are you treated at school?

53 How do you want to be treated?

54 What needs to change?

55 What are the potential benefits of conflict for learning and school life?

56 How does the school deal with conflict?

57 What can the school do to improve the way it deals with conflict?

58 How does the school support parents as their child's first and most important educator?

59 What support do parents appreciate most?

60 What else could the school do to support parents as educators?

61 How do parents know about what and how their children are learning?

62 How can parents learn about ways in which they can support their children's learning?

63 How does the school support teachers and other staff as learners?

64 What support for learning do staff appreciate most?

65 What else should the school do to support parents as learners?

66 What does the school community value about the governors?

67 How does the school support its governors as representatives and directors of the school community?

68 What support do the governors feel is most useful?

69 What else could the school do to support the role of governors?

70 How does the school enable all pupils to take part in running the school as a community?

71 What else could the school do to support pupil participation?

72 How does the school encourage and support lifelong learning in the community?

73 How many hours a day is the school open for learning?

74 How many hours a week is the school open for learning?

75 Out of 6,320 hours a year, how many are available for learning in school?

76 How could the school be more open and available for learning?

77 How does the local community contribute to learning and teaching?

78 What do young people value most from visitors and community involvement for learning?

79 What can be done to increase and improve community learning?

80 What contributions does the school make to the local community?

81 What do local people say about the school?

82 What contributions do local businesses make to the school?

83 What support does the school get from the Local Education Authority?

84 How does the school give feedback about the quality and nature of support from the LEA?

85 How can the LEA work best to support learning?

86 How do you use libraries, museums, sports centres or other places of learning in the community?

87 How could they improve the support they give for learning?

88 How could society increase recognition and support for their role in learning?

89 How do you use the Internet as a resource for learning?

90 What help and support do you want to improve your use of the Internet as a learning resource?

91 How does the school work with other services to improve the health, well-being, social cohesion, security, prosperity and environment of local people?

92 How do members of the school community give their views to elected representatives on the local council?

93 How do members of the school community hold elected representatives on the local council accountable for their policies and actions on education?

94 What are the central government's policies for education?

95 Which policies have helped improve learning and conditions for your school?

96 Which policies have not helped learning and conditions for your school?

97 Which policies have hindered learning and conditions for your school?

98 What is the single most useful change in government policy that you would recommend to improve the quality of learning for all?

99 What is the single most useful change in government policy you would recommend to increase *equality* in opportunities for learning?

100 How could local and national government recognise and encourage the achievement of schools as learning communities?

101 What can other schools learn from you about how to enhance learning and transform schools to meet the challenges of the twenty-first century?

Further resources

Education for a change

Global challenges

Alexander, Titus *Unravelling Global Apartheid: An overview of world politics* (Polity, 1996).

McGuire, Bill *A Guide to the End of the World* (OUP, 2003).

Rees, M. *Our Final Century: A Scientists Warning – How terror, error, and environmental disaster threaten humankind's future* (OUP, 2003).

Rischard, J. F. *High Noon: 20 global problems, 20 years to solve them* (Perseus, 2002).

Battle of ideas

Carnie, F., Large, M. and Tasker, M. (eds) *Freeing Education: Steps towards real choice and diversity in schools* (Hawthorn, Stroud, 1996).

Carnie, Fiona *Alternative Approaches to Education* (RoutledgeFalmer, 2002).

Gatto, John Taylor *Dumbing Us Down: The Hidden Curriculum of Compulsory Schooling* (New Society Publishers, Philadelphia, 1992).

Hargreaves, D. *Education Epidemic: transforming secondary schools through innovation networks* (DEMOS, London, 2003).

Hargreaves, D. *The Challenge for the Comprehensive School: culture, curriculum and community* (Routledge, London, 1982).

Tooley, J., Dixon P. and Stanfield, J. *Delivering Better Education: Market solutions for educational improvement* (Adam Smith Institute, 2003).

Tooley, J. *Reclaiming Education* (Cassell, London, 2000).

Woodhead, Chris *Class War: The State of British Education* (Little, Brown, London, 2002).

Department for education and skills

Innovation Unit website: www.standards.dfes.gov.uk/innovation-unit/

Investment for Reform and *Education and Skills: Delivering Results – A Strategy to 2006* (2001).

A New Specialist System: Transforming Secondary Education launched by Charles Clarke (2003).

Core Principles for Teaching and Learning, School Improvement and System-wide Reform (DfES Standards and Effectiveness Unit in February 2003).

Transforming Youth Work: Resourcing Excellent Youth Services (December 2002), sets out expectations of local authorities in co-ordinating and developing youth services.

The case for change

Parental involvement

Desforges, C. and Feinstein, L. *The Impact of Parental Involvement, Parental Support and Family Education on Pupil Achievement and Adjustment* (Ref: LEA/ 0339/2003). A downloadable DfES summary is on http://www.standards.dfes. gov.uk/studysupport/impact/parentalinvolvement/

Forms of intelligence

Claxton, Guy *Hare Brain, Tortoise Mind: Why intelligence increases when you think less* (Fourth Estate, London, 1997).

Goleman, D. *Emotional Intelligence: Why it can matter more than IQ* (Bloomsbury, London, 1996).

Gardner, H. *Intelligence Reframed: Multiple Intelligences for the 21st Century* (Basic Books, New York, 1999).

Going beyond the curriculum

Brighouse, T. *The Need to Go Beyond the National Curriculum* (RSA Journal, June 1996).

Design for learning

Bentley, Fairley and Wright *Design for Learning: Joined Up Design for Schools* (Demos/Sorrell Foundation, London, 2001).

The government case: every child matters

Every Child Matters: The Next Steps (DfES, 4 March 2004) summarised what had been said in consultation and setting out the Government's vision and plans. http://www.dfes.gov.uk/everychildmatters/downloads.cfm

School matters: learning matters

Brighouse, Tim and Woods, David *How to Improve Your School* (Routledge, London, 1999).

Mortimore, P. *et al. School Matters: the Junior Years* (Paul Chapman Publishing, 1988).

Sammons, P., Hillman, J. and Mortimore, P. *Key Characteristics of Effective Schools: A review of school effectiveness research* (Ofsted/Institute of Education, 1995).

A learning to learn school

Greany, T. and Rodd, J. *Creating a 'learning to learn' school: research and practice for raising standards, motivation and morale* (Network Educational Press, 2003).

The Campaign for Learning further research. See www.campaign-for-learning. org.uk

Senge, Peter *Schools that Learn: A Fifth Discipline Fieldbook for Educators, Parents and Everyone Who Cares About Education* (Nicholas Brealey, London, 2000).

Self-esteem and motivation

Further resources on Circle Time by Jenny Moseley: *Here We Go Round, Quality Circle Time for 3–5 year olds* (Positive Press); *Ring of Confidence: A Quality Circle Time Programme to Support Personal Safety for the Foundation Stage* (Positive Press); *Stepping Stones to Success: A Two Year Quality Circle Time Programme for Early Years* (Positive Press); *Quality Circle Time in the Secondary School* (David Fulton).

Further reading

Toward a State of Self-Esteem (California State Department of Education, Sacramento, 1990).

Lawrence, D. *Enhancing Self-esteem in the Classroom* (2nd edn, PCP Ltd, London, 1996).

Wetherall, M. and Maybin, J., in R. Stevens (ed.) *Understanding the Self* (Sage, London, 1996).

Burns, R. *Self-Concept Development and Education* (Holt Reinhart & Winston, London, 1982).

Owens, T., Stryker, S. and Goodman, N. *Extending Self-Esteem Research* (Cambridge University Press, Cambridge, 2001).

Emotional literacy

Bluestein, Jane *Creating Emotionally Safe Schools: A Guide for Educators and Parents* (Health Communications, Dearfield, Florida, 2001), www. janebluestein.com

Realising the Potential: Emotional Education for All (Antidote, London, 1997).

The Emotional Literacy Handbook (Antidote/David Fulton Publishers, 2003).

Damasio, A. R. *Descartes' Error. Emotion, Reason and the Human Brain* (Papermac, 1996).

LeDoux, J. *The Emotional Brain: The Mysterious Underpinnings of Emotional Life* (Weidenfeld & Nicolson, London, 1998).

Curriculum, schooling and the purpose of learning

Dalton, I., Fawcett, R. and West-Burnham, J. *Schools for the 21st Century* (Pearson Education/Secondary Heads' Association, Leicester, 2001).

DfES *Subject Specialism: Consultation Document* (DfES, London, 2003).

Breslin, T. *Chasing the Wrong Dream?* The quest for teacher professionalism and the emergence of the citizenship school, in Johnson, M. and Hallgarten, J., *From Victims of Change to Agents of Change: the future of the teaching profession* (Institute for Public Policy Research, London, 2002).

Breslin, T. Twenty years on: the great debate that never was, in Dainton, S. (ed.) *Take Care, Mr Blunkett: powerful voices in the new curriculum debate* (ATL, London, 1998).

Lucas, B. and Greany, T. *Schools in the Learning Age* (Campaign for Learning, London, 2000).

Ord, W. (2004) Philosophy for children: implications and opportunities for the citizenship classroom, in Breslin, T. and Dufour, B. (eds) *Developing Citizens: effective citizenship education in the secondary school social curriculum* (Kogan Page, London, 2004).

RSA Opening Minds (Royal Society of Arts, London, 2003).

White, John *et al. Rethinking the School Curriculum* (RoutledgeFalmer, London & New York, 2004).

E-learning

Castells, M. *The Internet Galaxy: Reflections on the Internet, Business and Society.* (Oxford, 2001).

Fulfilling the Potential: Transforming Teaching and Learning through ICT in schools. Downloadable pdf (DfES 2003) www.dfes.gov.uk/ictinschools

MORI, *Research into the attitudes and practices of secondary school pupils with regard to Information and Communications Technology (ICT)* (Campaign for Learning, 2002 – CfL).

Tests and exams

For updates on curriculum and examination reform (1–19 age group) go to http://www.14-19reform.gov.uk

Schools of the future

Bentley, Tom *Learning Beyond the Classroom* (Routledge, London, 1998).

DfES *Transforming Secondary Education* (DfES April 2003). Downloadable version at http://www.dfes.gov.uk/buildingonsuccess/secondary_education/viewsection.shtml

Crouch, C. *Commercialisation or Citizenship: Education Policy and the Future of Public Services* (Fabian Ideas 606, Fabian Society, March 2003).

Pring, R. E. and Walford, G. (eds) *Affirming the Comprehensive Ideal* (RoutledgeFalmer, London, 1997).

Benn, C. and Chitty, C. *Business, Business, Business : New Labour's Education Policy* (Tufnell Press, 1999).

Chitty, C., Benyon, J. (eds) *Education Policy in Britain* (Palgrave Macmillan, 2004).

Building schools for the future

http://www.teachernet.gov.uk/management/resourcesfinanceandbuilding/funding/bsf/ provides further information on this programme.

Extended and community schools

Got to http://www.teachernet.gov.uk/wholeschool/extendedschools/ for more information on Extended Schools.

Continyou is the national organisation that provides support for community education, go to http://www.continyou.org.uk/

CSV provides support for school community partnerships. http://www.csvcommunitypartners.org.uk/index.html?page=/home.html

Citizenship schools

Alexander, T. *Citizenship Schools: A Practical Guide* (Campaign for Learning/Southgate, 2001).

Campbell, J. Personal, Social and Health Education: Citizenship and the Whole Child, in Breslin, T. and Dufour, B. (eds) *Developing Citizens: effective citizenship education in the secondary school social curriculum* (Kogan Page, London, 2004).

Crick, B. (Chair) *Education for Citizenship and the Teaching of Democracy in Schools* (DfEE/QCA, London, 1998).

DfEE, *National Curriculum in Citizenship* (DfES, London, 2000).

Potter, J. *Active Citizenship in Schools: A Good Practice Guide to Developing a Whole School Policy* (CSV/Kogan Page, London, 2002).

Future schools

Further work by Tony Hinkley include: *The Deming Approach to School Improvement* (in *Improvement Through Inspection?*) (Fulton, 1996); *The School of the Future* (in *Schools in the Learning Age*) (Campaign for Learning, 2000); *Learning to Learn – engaging the ten percent* (in *21st Century Schools*) (Pearson, 2001); *If you were starting again will you start from here?* (in *Educational Leadership & the Community*) (Pearson, 2003).

Educators

Johnson, M. and Hallgarten, J. (2002) *From Victims of Change to Agents of Change: the future of the teaching profession* (Institute for Public Policy Research, London).

Deakin-Crick, R., Broadfoot, P. and Claxton, G. (2002) *Developing ELLI: The effective lifelong learning profile in practice* (Bristol, Lifelong Learning Foundation).

Deakin-Crick, R., Broadfoot, P. and Claxton, G. (2003a) Developing an Effective Lifelong Learning Inventory: The ELLI Project, *Assessment in Education,* forthcoming.

Deakin-Crick, R., Broadfoot, P. and Claxton, G. (2003b) Developing an Effective Lifelong Learning Inventory in Practice: the ELLI Project, forthcoming.

Glasser, W. (1993) *The Quality School Teacher* (HarperPerennial, NY).

Harlen, W. and Deakin-Crick, R. (2003) Testing and Motivation for Learning, *Assessment in Education,* forthcoming.

James, L. (2002) *Opening Minds Project Update* (London, Royal Society of Arts).

McCombs, B. L. P. (1997a) Development and validation of the learner-centred battery: Self-assessment tools for teacher reflection and professional development, *The Professional Educator*, 20, 1–20.

McCombs, B. W. J. (1997b) *The Learner Centred Classroom and School* (Jossey-Bass, San Francisco).

McGettrick, B. (2002) Transforming School Ethos: Transforming Learning Citizenship – Education in Action (Bristol University Graduate School of Education).

Rogers, C. (1994) *Freedom to Learn* (Merrill, Columbus, Ohio).

Engaging young people

Deming, W. E. *The New Economics: For Industry, Government, Education* (The MIT Press, 2000). Lipson Community College have adopted Deming's principles as the basis for their democratic commitment to excellence.

Hannam, D. *A pilot study to investigate the impact of the student participation aspects of the Citizenship Order on standards of education in secondary schools* (CSV Education, London, 2001).

School Councils and Pupil Exclusions: Research Project Report, Centre for International Education and Research (1998, 1999). School Councils UK

(London). Trafford, B. *Participation, power-sharing and school improvement*. (Education Heretics Press 1997); *Changemakers* is a national organisation focused on youth leadership and enterprise in school and youth settings. Go to http://www.changemakers.org.uk/; *School Councils UK* an organisation to promote student participation through school councils. Go to http://www.schoolcouncils.org/

Index